Phases &
Stages

D1602598

Terri Clark CDs:
Terri Clark
Just the Same
How I Feel
Fearless
Pain to Kill

Phases &
Stages

The
Terri Clark
Journals

INSOMNIAC PRESS

Edited by Catherine Jenkins
Copy edited by Adrienne Weiss
Cover and interior designed by Marijke Friesen

National Library of Canada Cataloguing in Publication Data

Clark, Terri
Phases & stages: the Terri Clark journals / Terri Clark.

ISBN 1-894663-56-X

1. Clark, Terri — Diaries. 2. Country musicians — Canada — Diaries.
I. Title. II. Title: Phases and stages. III. Title: Terri Clark journals.

ML420.C595A3 2003   782.421642'092   C2003-904142-5

The publisher gratefully acknowledges the support of the Canada Council, the Ontario Arts Council and the Department of Canadian Heritage through the Book Publishing Industry Development Program. We acknowledge the support of the Government of Ontario through the Ontario Media Development Corporation's Ontario Book Initiative.

Printed and bound in Canada

Insomniac Press
192 Spadina Avenue, Suite 403
Toronto, Ontario, Canada, M5T 2C2
www.insomniacpress.com

THE CANADA COUNCIL | LE CONSEIL DES ARTS
FOR THE ARTS | DU CANADA
SINCE 1957 | DEPUIS 1957

ONTARIO ARTS COUNCIL
CONSEIL DES ARTS DE L'ONTARIO

Introduction

These are the pages torn from a life. A life on the road, at home, and the ups and downs of it all. I started keeping a website journal a few years ago to gain insight into everyday living and have a record of events. Sometimes what is perceived by the public to be an easy, glamorous life, is not always what it seems. There's a lot of loneliness, wasted time on the highway, sacrifice, and thoughts of throwing in the towel to have a "normal life." But for 90 minutes every night, the power of music erases all of those feelings. I have truly been blessed. I spent my early years in Medicine Hat, Alberta, dreaming of this. Not of superstardom, limousines and Lear jets, but on a bus with 12 people who are as passionate about what music can bring as I am. I remember walking home from school and thinking to myself "where am I going to park the bus when I come home to visit mom?" I had it all planned out...just where there would be room to park my bus...I was 13. My family has long moved from that neighborhood, but I decided I had to do it anyway, and one day in 1996, much to the surprise of the people who have lived in that cul-de-sac for the past 30 years, we came driving up in a big shiny Silver Eagle bus, just to say I did it, and I found a place to park it, right in front of my childhood home. I am a big believer in dreams...I've been a dreamer most of my life. Nothing has come easy for me and there've been many ups and downs and hard work throughout the course of my career, but one thing is for certain...I wouldn't change a thing. We live in a world of judgment, and some may say I should have chosen differently, but the choices I've made in my life, both personally and professionally, will never leave me with regret. Not every album has sold a million copies, but I have been given the tremendous gift and responsibility of making music that matters and has an impact on people's lives, for the better. We must all follow our hearts and go where they lead us. I've learned so much about myself as a person and an artist over the past few years that it's the ones we reach who matter, the rest have their own paths to follow. I grew up listening to Reba McEntire, The Judds, Ricky Skaggs and Patsy Cline (to name a few). How their music changed my life and led me to where I am today, is something I cannot express enough. For God to have given me the same opportunity to impact others the way they did me, is the greatest gift of all. I'm glad to have the opportunity to share some of the daily highs and lows of my life with the people who mean the most to me. We are all here to make each other's lives richer and learn along the way, and I'm happy to share some of what I have learned in these pages.

 # December 26, 2000

Here I am in snowy Calgary, Alberta. It's the day after Christmas (what we call Boxing Day in Canada), and I have just experienced the most enlightening month of my life. It's funny how God will tap you on the shoulder to remind you where you should focus your energy in this life. It has been a stressful and emotional time dealing with the illness of my grandmother. We tend not to think of how fragile life can be, until it stares us in the face. Not only does illness or death have a great impact on our lives, but it forces us to be aware of our own mortality. I have seen an already close family become even closer during this time and realize how much support my grandparents have. I only hope someday to have the kind of children they do. It has been a bittersweet time for me, as I have finally had an opportunity to spend some quality time with family members I haven't seen much since I got my record deal. Life moves so fast. I have cousins who were little boys not long ago, who have become men, seemingly overnight. My music career has brought so much joy to my grandparents' lives, as they used to be professional musicians themselves. I continued on the journey that they started, and to hear the pride in my grandmother's voice as she introduces me as "Terri Clark, my granddaughter," makes every minute and every mile worthwhile. I got into the music business because I love music and have tremendous passion, but it has affected others in such a positive way, that now I see the REAL reason why. What good is talent if you can't share it? What good is a gift that is never opened?...It's funny how contemplative I've become since I've had the time to stop and think. Hopefully my grandmother will be well enough to come home and lead a somewhat comfortable life...she may be with us for 2 weeks, 2 months, or 10 years...whenever her time is up, but isn't that true for all of us? Life is so short, and we have much to learn in so little time, I hope I never stop learning.

Terri

 # January 1, 2001

Here I am in the year 2001. There were times, as a child, when I thought that sounded so far away. I figured we'd all be flying our cars through the air with high-powered space engines and live in the land of "The Jetsons" by now. I guess the more things change, the more they stay the same. However, when you think of the progress the world has made since they rang in the year 1901, it really is mind-boggling...can you imagine being a hundred years old, having actually gone through the changes that have taken place in society and technology?...It's fun to sit and ponder the different ways one has spent New Year's Eves of the past...how much life has changed, yet how much it really hasn't. We are who we are born to be. I think our morals and values will always be the same, just the circumstances under which we live will be ever-changing. I looked around at the many wonderful people I rang in this New Year with and was so thankful for the love that has blessed my life. One more year has gone by and one more page has turned. What should I do to make this year different than all the others that came before?...Isn't that something we all ask ourselves? I really don't know the answer, but I feel like every year I'm still breathing is one more opportunity to try and make a difference. Music allows me a voice and a forum to bring joy to others' lives, and I'm ever so grateful for that ability. I guess what I want for the New Year is to keep growing and learning. As long as we're doing these two things, we're making progress.

On another note...I've found that my dog Oscar is a celebrity. When we go out in public, people ask, "Hey, who's that chick with Oscar?" He certainly lights up a room...he must be a Leo! (I really don't know his sign, as I adopted him from the pound when he was two.) Being a Leo myself, I know we all love an audience...He immediately starts putting on the Ritz for all who have the honour of basking in his presence. It's so funny to watch him sit up and beg for attention...he looks like a cocktail waiter in a five-star restaurant. People were ordering martinis from him at the New Year's Eve party. He had trouble carrying the tray (I think he just drank too much punch).

My grandmother is having good and bad days, but they seem hopeful that she may come home soon. I'm glad to be home, so I can imagine it's been really hard for her being in the hospital for 2 months!!!! Makes me so grateful for good health. Until next time...

January 5, 2001

Well, yesterday was quite eventful for me and my friend Tonda. We both had the day off, so we decided to do some things we don't usually do, since we don't see each other that much. She's been on a Patsy Cline kick lately, and announced to me that we were going to look for Patsy's old house in Goodletsville. Every time she stopped the car and asked someone where Patsy's house was, I nearly crawled under the seat. These people, of course, looked at us like we were out of our minds and weren't much help at all. We do think we found it though...I don't know who lives there now, but it was all I could do to keep Tonda from peeking in the windows and getting us arrested. Thelma and Louise...LOOK OUT! Then after that, Tonda decides we're going to go to Tootsie's Orchid Lounge (she's never been there). We walk into a mostly empty place at about 4 p.m., and ended up having the time of our lives. We must have stayed until 9 p.m. or so. I was up singing with the band every chance I got (take a wild guess...Patsy Cline songs, per Tonda's request).

Anyway, I met some really nice people and by the time we left, the place was jam-packed. It's a good thing Tonda had a husband and child waiting at home, or I would never have left. It's funny how the memories of playing in that place came flooding back. I realize how fortunate I have been in music. Thirteen years ago I sat at that bar and dreamed of one day going to the awards shows, as I watched the limos drive by the front window. I guess it goes to show anything can happen and dreams really do come true!

January 7, 2001

Well Tonda and I did it again. We took her daughter and my niece to Chuck E. Cheese's yesterday for almost three hours. I've never been there, but discovered it's a great way to keep kids occupied so that YOU can have ALL the pizza to yourself...they never sit down! I got asked out by the guy in the mouse suit...me dating a mouse, well THAT ought to get the media's attention! Then the kids both fell asleep in the middle of the movie *102 Dalmatians* and we were stuck there watching a movie neither of us gave a hoot about...the popcorn was good though! She and I have made up for a lot of lost time this past week! Today I went to my first Titans game. Of course the one game I go to, they end up losing...I hope I wasn't a jinx...I'm not a huge sports fan, but must admit I got into the game, once someone explained to me what was going on.

(P.S. Today my Nanny got to go home...those prayers must have worked...)

January 10, 2001

Whenever I have time to sit still, I realize just how much a "normal" life can be just as fulfilling as a life on the road. I love playing music for people so much and am glad that having that kind of balance is something I'm finally learning. Having some time off has been a crucial thing for me, as I'm about to embark on a very busy season of touring. I'm very excited to get back out there and play in Canada. It's been too long since I toured here and many folks haven't seen the new show at all. I love doing the acoustic sets just as much as the full band shows, as they give me an opportunity for a more relaxed atmosphere and the chance to talk more about songwriting, as well as really keep up my guitar playing skills.

On another note…As soon as my grandmother started to recover and came home from the hospital, I got a phone call that my grandfather on my dad's side is now very ill. It seems these things tend to happen all at the same time, but there isn't really much we can do when age sets in. It really is an awakening, however, when you start to see a generation (not that far removed from your own) start to disappear. No matter what happens, I have been so blessed to have all my grandparents live as long as they have and know that a lot of people my age haven't been as lucky. We must always tell those we love how we feel today...we may not have tomorrow.

January 12, 2001

Wow, what an eventful weekend I had! I went back out on the road to do what we call "makeup" dates in Georgia and Florida…these are the dates I had to cancel last month. It was so great to get back up on stage with all the guys again, as this will be the last full band show until the end of May. We're currently gearing up for an extensive acoustic "unplugged" tour. I loved the electricity in the two clubs we played, but was disturbed at some of the events. The first show was a bigger venue than the second and the audience seemed a little more comfortable. However, after the show, I was disturbed at the sight of a girl backstage having severe convulsions from drinking too much. It wasn't my fault, although my conscience made me feel some responsibility, as it was my show she was attending. I've seen some detrimental effects alcohol can have on people and hope that it never directly touches my life in such a negative way. I'm glad folks have a good time at the shows, but hope everyone is careful where that stuff is concerned. Anyway, the paramedics came and she ended up being okay, after scaring the living daylights out of everyone back there…including me. The second show in Tampa was by no means a drag. We had their largest crowd ever…but I know many people got bad placement, couldn't see or hear, and it was clearly packed to the point of being a serious fire hazard…if someone had decided to light a match, several people would have died trying to get out…I also would hate to see how they would've removed someone if they were having a heart attack or something.

One of our band members was absent over the weekend, so I covered his acoustic parts on the guitar Saturday night, which I really enjoyed, since I usually play so much electric during the show. The crowds were great and enthusiastic, and since I couldn't play cowbell on "Poor Pitiful Me" (I was playing guitar), I called one of my loyal fans up onstage to do it…she nearly put a hole in the cowbell, but I do believe a star was born! A good time was had by all. I met some great guys on my golf team in Orlando…had the best time ever. I don't know if I was planning on having so much fun, but I did. I don't golf, so I pretty much stuck to driving the cart. A spokesperson from The Ronald McDonald Foundation rode with me…I think she should get an award for being the most COURAGEOUS! That cart should have been four-wheel drive, the way I was driving it.

I had a fun weekend and came home to the news that my grandfather is full of cancer and we don't know how long he has left. I'm going to see him for a day before the tour starts...life is short...

 # January 28, 2001

Boy, it sure has been a hectic couple of weeks. We played the Grand Ole Opry last weekend and had such a blast. Jeff played upright acoustic bass and we did a bluegrass ensemble Friday night. I just loved every minute of it. The feeling of tradition in the Ryman Auditorium is overwhelming and it certainly holds a distinct, almost "spooky" mystique. I'm such a fan of honest music, which includes bluegrass, folk, rock, and raw country, and there is no better place to hear it than in that building. I always get so nervous playing the Opry...maybe 'cause I want to make those who have come before me proud. Looking backstage from the spotlight, I see Little Jimmy Dickens, Bill Anderson and John Conlee all watching me sing...wow!...Sometimes I wonder how on earth I got here and what I did to deserve such a wonderful dream coming true.

We rehearsed for our acoustic tour over at my house. Our friend Annette brought lots of goodies for us to snack on and great food that she cooked. We put together a very nice show and included some oldies from the first 3 albums that never made it to radio. Some of my favorite songs tend to be album cuts. The "No Fear" video got "Pick Hit" at CMT and I was thrilled to learn that early indicators at radio are really good. I hope and pray that this song gets heard by as many people as possible, as I feel it is a strong message that will help spread good energy. We did our first acoustic show in Denver and it went really well...other than a couple of clams from me on my guitar (first show jitters)...the crowd was great and I loved the venue. The next morning I woke up at the hotel feeling like I was coming down with a cold...did radio interviews, then flew to Salt Lake City for a sound check, then the show that night. By the end of that show I wasn't feeling too hot...but was told that the dryness of the air and altitude might be the cause of my funk...I think they were right, as I'm now feeling a bit better.

I'm flying to Canada for one night to say my last goodbyes to my grandfather, as he is now in the terminal unit at the hospital. It won't be easy, and this is the first time this has happened in my family. From there I'm off to Portland, and the tour really begins, with no break until Feb 26th. I've been nominated for two Juno awards (Canada's Grammy equivalent)...in two categories: "Best Female Artist" and "Best Country Female"...apparently it's unusual for a country artist to be in the former category, and I appear to be the only one this year. I'm up against my buddy Jann Arden...that's gonna be a tough one to beat. She's an amazing artist. I'm looking forward to what the next few months hold in store for me. I thank God every day for blessing me with such a full, wonderful life, and wonderful family, friends and fans...what more could a girl want?

Calgary, Alberta, April 4, 2003
Photographer: Jim Wells

Edmonton, Alberta, April 1, 2003
Photographer: Jim Wells

Calgary, Alberta, April 4, 2003
Photographer: Jim Wells

Calgary, Alberta, April 4, 2003
Photographer: Jim Wells

February 1, 2001

Well, this has been quite a week for me. My Grandad passed away last night. I was so lucky to have had the chance to say "goodbye" to him before he made his journey to the next place. I had less than 24 hours to fly to Canada, see him, then fly all the way to Oregon for the first acoustic show. I ended up getting ill, but all of the travelling was worth that last chance to see him look at me and know that he was aware that I had come to see him one last time. I'm feeling better now, but I was really afraid I was going to be cancelling shows…I just took it easy, shortened the sets a bit, and sang a little "lighter." I guess it must be hard for people to understand why I don't always come out to sign autographs after shows, but this week was just not a good one for me. I always feel guilty about not giving everything I can all the time, but I realize as I get older, that I'm human, and sometimes all I have in me is the energy to put on the best show I can, so I try to honor where I'm at.

I'm looking forward to starting the first show of our Canadian "unplugged" tour tonight. We're in Nanaimo, B.C. right now…a quaint little fishing community…what a real treat. Had some great Japanese food for lunch. I miss Canada so much when I come back home, and really feel my roots more and more the older I get.

I filmed a piece for the show "America's Most Wanted" yesterday in Seattle. A friend of mine who works for Mercury Records lost an uncle last summer. His life was taken by one of the ranch hands he'd hired. The family had tried to get the show involved to see if they could aid in the capture of his assailant…to no avail. When I was told that they would do it if I got involved (they wanted celebrity involvement)…I didn't hesitate. It felt great to be able to help, and I realize how fortunate I am that such senseless tragedy has never touched my family. It's time to move forward now and enjoy life and the gifts we are all given. I know that I have had many wonderful people praying for my family the past few months and it is something I feel very grateful and blessed for.

February 13, 2001

Well, well, well…it certainly has been a hectic time for me lately. It's wonderful being back in Canada, "my home and native land." Every time I tour or come to visit, I always get this little pang in my heart. I don't know if it's just the "Swiss Chalet cravings," or what…(that's my favorite place to eat here). Seriously, I guess no matter where you go, you always feel your "roots" when you go home. "ROOTS"…it's actually a popular Canadian casual sports clothing line, which I LOVE!

The tour has been sold out in every market, and we've had great reviews and much success thus far with the "unplugged" show. We're doing a few select acoustic dates in the States too, so I hope the fans who've come out to all of the "electric" shows will dig this as much as we are digging doing them. It's so nice to just sit there, say what's on my mind, talk about song-writing, and be a real musician…it's great fun. "No Fear" is being received very well on both sides of the border also. Life couldn't be much better right now. The song jumped 18 spaces on the Canadian chart last week (42-24)! I was in shock, but very delighted. The American charts take MUCH longer (5-6 months), but they will get there. I hope the message of the song reaches far and wide, if nothing else.

Looks like the TCFC party may be at Tootsie's this year…it's a smaller space, but we all thought the nostalgia would make for a really neat atmosphere. I've been away from home for a few weeks now and find myself getting a little "road weary." I still have a long way to go, but I miss domesticity sometimes. I love my road crew and band so much, that they're really easy to be around…thank God, since we're all crammed on one bus together for these two months. I'm just so thankful to be able to get up every day and enjoy what makes my living…not everyone can say that. My mom came to the show last night. It was a good show for me, pacing went well. Sometimes I tend to spend too much time talking, not enough time singing…oh well, I guess I just gotta go with it. It's Valentines Day tomorrow…I anticipate getting some chocolate thrown at me tomorrow night at the show (just what I DON'T need) People have been bringing me cigars and beer…I don't really smoke cigars, but I need to find someone who does.

Jann Arden and I got together in Calgary to rehearse for the Juno awards (we're doing a tribute to Bruce Cockburn…a well-known

Canadian folk artist)...I'm excited about singing with her on TV...it will help us not be as nervous to do the song together.

I got to visit my Nanny again too. I can't believe how well she is doing...If someone had told me two months ago she would be getting around this well, I would've thought they were dreaming...it has truly been a miracle...all those prayers worked...I swear they did. Prayer is such a powerful way to heal...amazing energy. After losing my Grandad, I am so grateful for, and cherish every moment with, my other grandparents.

We have to travel a long way tonight...there isn't too much snow, so it should be safe travelling. Our biggest worry was getting through the mountains in British Columbia and that part of the tour is finished, so it shouldn't be too hard from here on out. You still can't help but wake up every time the brakes are hit...it's just a reflex. We travel overnight most of the time, so I'm asleep until we get to the next town (*if* I sleep)...it takes getting used to, but after the first week, I get into a groove and it's not too hard. I've had the odd day off, and been in some places where I can hook up with old high school buddies and family, which has been great. I'm spending today with my mom and dad. We're having big grilled steaks for dinner (mmmmm), then they are taking me to the bus, so we can go on to Grande Prairie, Alberta tonight...on the road again!!!

February 21, 2001

5 more days and I get to go home...yipeeeeee! I will have 2 whole days off before I head into CRS. The big Country radio seminar in Nashville. It keeps us all hopping, but gives us a chance to schmooze with the radio people who play the music (or not)... Anyway, after that, I go to Georgia, then to Toronto for the Juno awards, then back onto the second leg of the Canadian acoustic tour. My tour manager told me that there were 4 people at last night's show who called before the show started, wanting their money back, because they found out it was an "acoustic" show and they wanted the full band electric show. The promoter told them to go to the show, and if they were disappointed, he would give them their money back...no one showed up after the show to get their money back...(hmm, guess it weren't so bad after all). We're having such a blast, but I can tell the road is wearing a bit on everyone. It's only natural. Sometimes all it takes is a few days to sleep in your own bed and stand on your own turf, then it's time to go play

again...We love what we do, that makes the time away so worthwhile. I'm looking forward to the rest of this year. I think it's going to be a good one. I'm excited to see how "No Fear" and "Empty" do for me on the radio and in album sales. I guess this one is so personal, it's something I hope gets heard. I'm having second thoughts about holding the TCFC party at Tootsie's...we're exploring other options. I'm just concerned about the limited space and heat in June...UGH! It would be a blast, but for a group of maybe 100 people, not 400. Time to give Oscar a bath. He LOVES that (yeah RIGHT!!!)

February 27, 2001

Here I am, finally at home, and I'm really enjoying myself. The shows have all gone so well, so far, and I'm looking forward to our next Canadian run. The video for "No Fear" is doing great, as is the song. I'm so glad that the Canadian Special Olympics asked me to do the video. It was so wonderful that they found "No Fear" a great song to base their inspirational footage around. We actually thought it was just going to be a video for the Special Olympics to play at the games, but it turned into so much more when we all saw it. I guess people all have their opinions and that's something we must honor. It's hurtful, and hard to read some of the things on the Internet, partly because I feel that I go out of my way to be friendly 99% of the time…but there's always that 1% that gets us in trouble—and after all we're all human. I will try not to beat myself up…All we can do is be ourselves, work hard, and have unconditional love for our fellow beings; it works both ways. That is the thought of the day.

March 8, 2001

Wow, I've had quite the week. I got home and started my CRS schedule (radio seminar). I got to see many familiar faces I've come to know over the past 6 years. It's really interesting to see all the new artists attending for the first time, going through all the interviews and shows. I guess it makes me feel a bit old. Somebody called me a "veteran" the other day and it scared the daylights out of me. Saturday I went to Valdosta, Georgia to do the acoustic show. It was the first time we'd played that particular venue, and it was daylight, so we couldn't really get candles and incense going, but the crowd was very attentive and kind. It was great to see familiar faces in the audience there too. I flew out of Atlanta on Sunday to perform/attend the Juno awards in Toronto, Ontario. I flew directly to Toronto and the show went live to air that very night. Of course the airline lost my bag with all my awards show gear in it and I almost had a heart attack. They eventually found it and it got to me about an hour before the show started. I really think God is testing me sometimes, since I'm not the most patient person in the world…that was the ultimate challenge on that day. I ended up winning best female country artist, which was such a thrill. It's been ages since I walked up the stairs to get an award and it felt great. I try not to let awards dictate how I feel about myself or my music, but it really was nice to get recognized this year. The performance with Jann Arden went better than expected and it was a real honor to be up on that stage with such a talented artist. I got to spend some time with family in Toronto after the show, so it was a pleasurable few days. I just flew into Halifax, and will be doing 3 interviews for TV in a few minutes, so I had better go get my "face" on now…more later.

March 22, 2001

We just crossed the border back into the US! The Canadian tour was a complete success and I'm thrilled with the feedback on our "unplugged" shows. We did a live multi-track recording of the Toronto show (the last one) and may possibly be able to use it for various things in the future. The crowd was exceptional that night and we had a great time. I'm looking forward to the last few shows here on the other side of the border. We'll be in Detroit tonight, then on to Cincinnati, Indy and St. Louis. I'm looking forward to seeing some familiar faces in the audience. My bedtime reading last night was a bunch of really nice cards from some really nice folks, that were given to me at a show recently. Feel the love?…oh yes.

Time off is going to be well needed and I'm so looking forward to cooking in my own kitchen, sleeping in my own bed, and all of those normal domestic treasures. I'm going to try to figure out how to grow garlic. It could be a total disaster, but I keep buying out the garlic at Kroger, as I use tons of it in my cooking. They say it helps ward off colds…maybe that's why I hardly ever get sick. It may also be why nobody comes within ten feet of me after I eat one of my own meals.

Oscar will probably be so confused regarding his whereabouts, he may poop all over the house. He's bus trained beyond belief at this point, and after 2 months straight living on one, he may rebel. I guess I will just have to prepare for the worst and arm myself with plenty of pooper scoopers.

I've decided to take up rollerblading again soon. This time with a helmet…everyone has told me I'm forbidden to skate without one. Since my shoulder surgery, I've been very cautious of doing things like that, but have decided it's one of the only forms of exercise I really enjoy, so what the hell, I'm going for it. Until next time…

April 3, 2001

Well, I guess all of this time off has made me lazy about writing in my diary here. How nice it's been to get back to some normal things in life. I've been busy using the bag of garlic one of my oh-so-thoughtful fans gave me at a show not long ago. Maybe it was that last entry that gave her the idea?...hmmmmmm. I've been walking, and rollerblading, and getting massages, and watching movies, and cooking for friends, and visiting with mom. She's staying with me for a couple of weeks. She helps me so much with my business affairs, I don't know what I'd do without her! Oscar has been a very good boy and we have taken some really nice long walks in the wonderful parks around town. My last few "unplugged" shows went well...not all of the venues were desirable, but hey, I'm just glad there were people there!

I just got a rough CD of the live "unplugged" show we recorded at the Trinity Church in Toronto. We're all so pleased with the way it sounds, you never know what might come of it. We're discussing some options. It was such an electrifying night and the crowd was so enthusiastic, the band and I were all at our best, and it was captured on tape beautifully.

I called a radio station in Tampa this morning and surprised Mary Chapin Carpenter on the air, as she was their morning show guest...I was still half asleep, but it was a blast.

"No Fear" is doing well, slowly but surely...I will keep saying a prayer that it continues to grow and flourish. Phone requests certainly are of the essence (hint, hint). I saw some really nice folks in Indianapolis. We had a nice time chatting from the bus window, while being serenaded by a harmonica-playing Bob Dylan wannabe. I gave him a bottle of wine as payment for his entertainment services. We're so excited to be playing the Fillmore in San Francisco next month. It's a historical place and I feel like it will be a special evening for us, also the first run with the full band. I have a new guitar player and drummer starting in May, so it'll be a neat thing for them to be a part of right off the bat. Well, mother is calling me for dinner, so I had better not keep her waiting...till next time...

 # April 14, 2001

Well, the webcast went great the other night. I must say the guys and I were all pretty nervous, knowing that the exposure was huge and how many people were watching. Saw some familiar faces in the crowd, one of whom asked me a question. Those questions are a bit awkward. You never know what to expect, however nobody asked me anything weird, like what kind of underwear I had on or something like that. I had a great time, and by the end of the show, we had all loosened up quite a bit. I have the greatest fans in the world, and it was great to know they all tuned in (or at least tried to), even from Canada.

I'm getting my war paint on to go out on the town with Tonda tonight...God only knows what trouble we'll get into this time. I expect we'll have a good time, as there's never a dull moment with us. "No Fear" is doing better each week and is currently up to #24 in R&R...I pray it continues to grow. We're looking forward to the summer tour and the fan club party. We have some really cool new jackets I just saw today. Ummmm…mom had a great visit, but was ready to get home, as we all are after a long time away. Easter is upon us and I'm just going to relax this weekend, as we had our family gathering last weekend (since mom was here to cook the turkey!!!) Until next time…

May 1, 2001

I just got back on Sunday from my little trip. I went to New York City first to an audition for a commercial and then off to Barbados. I had a wonderful time there. The director of tourism (Rob) had a great time with me and my crazy friends, and we'll stay in touch for a long time, I'm sure…he was a very helpful sweet guy. I managed not to burn myself and came home with a Coppertone tan. After eating (and drinking) at an all-inclusive resort for a week, one needs all the help one can get…you know what I mean? They say a tan makes you look slimmer…BRING IT ON! I went jet skiing with some nice folks from Alberta and B.C. who won the CMT contest. Snorkelling was fabulous, and for the first time I wasn't afraid of what might be coming up behind me. Barbados is a pretty conservative British commonwealth country, so we had to wear long pants to dinner every night. I didn't bring many, so my parachute pants had to do. People were looking at me like "who let that classy broad in here?" I guess it's come to be expected…I hate to dress up for anything…it's uncomfortable and takes too much time. I had lamb one night for dinner (which was GREAT). The restaurant at the resort rocked. Jason McCoy and Paul Brandt were a blast too. I went to a big tourist thing with Paul and his wife one day, a big cave. Then we spent a long time getting lost (we did a lot of backing up). I ate sugar cane right from the stem, mmm good. I did a show in Miami on Saturday, so instead of flying home, then back, I just stayed in Miami for 2 days before coming home. South Beach is always an adventure. This morning I got up at 6 a.m. to do a live satellite radio tour of 24 stations. We really need to get "No Fear" pumping now, as it's just barely stayed alive the past few weeks. Requests and listener passion will help a lot. I have faith that we will persevere, but it's scary at times…No Fear right? I'm getting ready for band rehearsals and we'll be hitting the road with the live full band show mid-May…we are excited to have 2 new band members…one is a guitarist from Newfoundland named Craig Young. I've never had a Canadian in the band and it is about TIME! Well, I suppose I should go get my laundry finished from the trip…there's sand everywhere…

 # May 5, 2001

What a week…I guess I don't even need to go into the reason why, I believe it's been given enough attention. All I can hope is that some good comes out of this situation and I know that God gives challenges us for a reason. A way for us to grow as individuals and to send a message to others. If the events of the past week will make one person stop and think before doing something they shouldn't, then it's a positive, as far as I can see. Sometimes we look at things selfishly, and only think of the pain and embarrassment that has been caused to us as individuals, instead of looking at the whole picture. Sometimes one person's pain can save another person's life. Pain is necessary for spiritual and emotional growth. I only wish that when the media chooses to report a story, they would focus as much on the positive ones, as they do on the negative. When a public figure goes virtually without any media attention until they do something wrong, it just doesn't seem right. Especially in light of the fact that so many positive things in the past have gone unreported or noticed and not gotten half the attention. I regret that the Canadian media has misreported this story in many ways and already convicted me...they were the one's who I thought would at least give me the benefit of the doubt and a chance to comment before running it like a tabloid story. Enough about that.

I've been invited to be on the ACM awards on Wednesday night...I can't say what part of the show yet, as it's a special surprise to another performer, but I'm excited and thrilled to be a part of it. I've always admired this performer and am glad I will get to go and be a part of this.

The Sugarbugs event went very well last night. I sang a Patsy Cline song with a young lady who bid in an auction to sing a song on stage with me...she was pretty darn good too!! No matter what happens with "No Fear," I am so glad that organizations such as this and the Special Olympics have found the inspiration behind this song and adopted it as the slogan song for the organizations. We need requests and passion at radio for the song now more than ever, as we're teetering on a weekly basis and hitting a hard spot with it. I'm so looking forward to getting back on the road and playing to the people who pay my check...music heals the heart!

May 23, 2001

Well, here we are in California (God, I love it here). These very well may be my favorite crowds in the US, they're all as crazy as I am. Speaking of crazy...we played the Crazy Horse in Irvine Sunday night and I fell absolutely madly in love. He was the cutest thing I've ever seen. Red hair, 4 legs and cute droopy ears. He was a 7-week-old Dachshund puppy. I adopted Oscar from the pound, so I never got to see him as a puppy, so, as you can imagine, this one just stole my heart. He belonged to the lead singer in the opening band and I don't think she saw her puppy till we left, 'cause I had him all day. It would be great to get another dog, but I just travel too much for that right now...but someday I will.

Boy, was I ever exhausted after this weekend. I did a show in Victorville, California, Thursday night, Porterville, California, Friday night, then flew to Edmonton, Alberta at 6 a.m. Saturday morning, did the benefit show with Jann Arden that night, then flew to L.A. on Sunday morning, drove to Irvine, and played there that night. I am spent.

I did a bunch of shopping in L.A. today. I bought a pair of camouflage pants, I've always wanted some. There's a cool thrift store I go to on Melrose and it has neat used clothes. I like used clothes; they're cheap and already worn in. I wonder if I'm wearing dead people's clothes?...was that out loud?...Sorry, I guess I should try not to think about that right?

Umm...oh yeah, I was paging through *People Magazine*, and what to my wandering eyes does appear? ME right there smack dab in the middle of the ACM page. Never thought I'd get a picture that big in *People Magazine*...I thought it was pretty cool and made me feel a lot better in light of the fact that "No Fear" has stalled on the charts. What a disappointment...but I won't let it get me down. "Getting There" is slated to be released at the end of June. I think it's a good choice and we've been opening the shows with it for a year now.

I was in Borders music in L.A. and noticed that I was the only "Clark" in the country section without an I.D. card. Guy Clark, Roy Clark and Floyd Cramer had their own cards, but I didn't...my album was pushed back behind all the others. So, being the fearless one that I am, I go up to the attendant and say, "How come Terri Clark doesn't have a card?" He goes, "Well, I guess he doesn't have as many albums as the others do"...and I said, "That he, is ME, and I have 4 albums out." Anyway, my friend was laughing her butt off at me and I was trying to convince this salesperson I deserved my own name card like everyone else. I think he thought I was some deranged street person who just wandered in to cause a scene. I found the *People Magazine* right after that and had to restrain myself from shoving it in his face…it was pretty hilarious. I guess that's about all the adventurous stuff I can muster up for today…I've seen some familiar faces at the shows out here and we've had a great time…more to come…

May 27, 2001

I logged on to a fan-oriented web page tonight. I entered a chatroom, and boy it's amazing how much time I spent defending the fact that it was really me. It must mean there are a lot of impostors out there, however I would hope those people have better things to do with their time than impersonate me on a webpage... I had a great time and found the experience to be refreshing in light of the fact that I was speaking through a modem so it's less personal. I think it's certainly an effective way of getting to know people for people, as it puts us all on the same level, instead of in a meet and greet autograph line, or a "I'm the fan, you're the star" atmosphere...I guess if I was a doctor, saving lives or inventing cures for diseases, I'd feel more deserving of such adoration, but it's so sweet and nice to know the music goes appreciated...what fun. Until next time...

June 7, 2001

Well, here I am back home (finally). I've had a very relaxing week of R & R. Took a long drive out in the country to get away from the phone, fax and computer. Sometimes it's important for us to be alone, with ourselves and our thoughts. Nature is the best way to get back in touch with my center, and get my feet back on the ground. This summer will be very busy for me, starting with fan fair next week. I did some interviews for some upcoming shows this morning and a couple of them played "Getting There"...that was cool. It really does sound pretty good on the radio...hopefully this one will do well. I'm looking forward to the fan club party next week...I think I'm going to do the acoustic show, for those who haven't yet had an opportunity to see it. It will be rusty, as we haven't done it since March, but I'm sure the errors will be forgiven...there's always a lot of love in the room. The Planet Hollywood chat was interesting...I was logged on-line at the same time I was dictating my answers, so I was able to see what the conversation was as it was going on. It was nice to be able to talk directly with everyone. I'm packing right now, getting ready for the weekend trip. Oscar is looking at me with that "face" that says..."I hope you're taking me with you this time." Whenever he sees me packing, he knows what's going on...now THAT is scary. I got a new Telecaster relic guitar for the shows this year...and I'm thoroughly enjoying playing it...it really sounds better than any I've had and is an exact replica of a 1963 model...rusty bridge and all...gotta love it...makes me feel like ROCKIN'. Well, better get back to the packing...

June 30, 2001

As I write this journal entry, I'm sitting in a motel room that will NEVER be mistaken for the Ritz Carlton. I swear, if people only knew just how UN-glamorous this can be sometimes, they would be amazed. I have a phone and cable, which is good, but the water is brown, which is bad. Good thing we aren't staying overnight, I'm afraid of what might be in the bed. We stayed at the nicest resort/casino in Michigan. It's called the Soaring Eagle. I swear it's the best we've ever been treated at a casino and we loved it. Kevin dropped his dobro during the bluegrass segment and it made the loudest CRASH! I turned around to see him standing there with the combination of shock and bewilderment on his face. I couldn't finish the song, as I was laughing too hard to sing, and Robbie was left hanging on a few notes, when I quit in the middle of a line. All in all, it was a fun show, and I would go back there in a second. "Getting There" is getting there...lots of airplay in Canada and seems to be getting good response here in the US as well. Songs take so long to kick in these days that it will be a while before we know about doing a video. We're getting some good outlines and ideas ready now, so we're set to go when the time comes.

I'm looking forward to the rest of the summer. We have a lot of gigs booked and I'm happy to be getting all the work that I want. I'm going to Canada to visit with family on my vacation, it will be so beautiful there this time of year. I took my niece to see *Shrek*…what a hoot. I loved the message it set forth, to love people for who they are on the inside. I might actually go and see it again. This year I will be home for the 4th of July for the first time in years. I will try not to catch myself on fire with any fireworks…okay, well, maybe I should just avoid the fireworks all together…

I'm sitting here watching TV, and I swear, not a commercial goes by without seeing "Miss Cleo and her free psychic readings"…SOMEONE is making some money. If I had only known, all I had to do to get more TV time is read Tarot cards, well, I would have been HUGE by now. Those commercials are really starting to get on my nerves…who calls those things anyway?

July 21, 2001

I had an amazing time at the Exit Inn in Nashville last Thursday night. It was incredibly hot in there, and I felt so bad for the people who were sandwiched in together in the room, but believe me, it was twice as hot on that stage. I swear to God, I literally felt light-headed for a minute or two, and was afraid I would end up face down at one point. I had one of the best shows I've had so far this year and was thrilled with the fan and industry turnout. I decided to play Nashville, as it's been years (if ever) since we've done a full show there. Sometimes I think Nashville gets ignored by a lot of mainstream artists, because we live there, but it's important for the community that we not forget that Nashville is a market where people live, work, and buy records, as well as a lot of music lovers live in Nashville. I had a great time, and plan on doing it again in the future. The Exit Inn was a good place, as they're known for having great sound, and I've seen many of my favorites play there. Air conditioning would have been nice, but hey, it went well just the same.

Speaking of *Just the Same*...the prez of my label gave me a platinum plaque for that album. That puts my sales worldwide at close to 4 million so far. Hard to believe that many people have gone and plunked down their hard earned change for one of my records...makes me sooooooo thankful and grateful.

There was a mix-up about a radio station visit the day of the show. Apparently the station thought I was coming and I wasn't supposed to, so they announced it and had to go back and say they'd made a mistake...all of this was completely beyond me and I heard about it that afternoon...I guess there's a first time for everything.

I'm playing "Jamboree in the Hills" today...these shows are really making me sweat off that 15 lbs I needed to lose...I'm shrinking before my very eyes. I got a new tattoo on my vacation...YEP!!!!...A red Canadian Maple leaf on my right shoulder. If that ain't pride, I don't know what is...I am so proud to be a Canadian and have now branded myself for life. It must be me fighting the fact that I'm going to be 33 soon...YYYYYYYYUCK!!!!! I think tattoos and fast cars are the way we hold onto our youth...next, it's the fast car.

August 1, 2001

Holy Moses, do I feel like I've been running a marathon or WHAT? We've been so busy lately, it's amazing...good, but tough as H-E-double hockey sticks. I've been in New York City a lot lately, 'cause we've been doing a few shows in the area, and I went to the David Letterman show on Monday night. After years of managers and publicists trying to get me on the show, I finally made my debut...as a seat-filler. Yep!!!!...they sat us in the nosebleed section in these folding chairs (like I used to have when my kitchen table was a card table), and told us we were given free tickets so that we would be the designated people to sit in the seats that the audience members left empty when they got up. WELL, let me just say this, it was the last thing I thought I would be doing the first time I was in that TV studio...a humbling experience indeed. One of the security guards looked at me, and said "Don't I know you? You look sooooo familiar"...then he said, "Aren't you a pro-basketball player?"

I found out yesterday I'm nominated for 6

CCMA awards. I was so thrilled to hear about that and couldn't believe it. I'm not going into this expecting anything, that way I won't be let down if I don't win, but I was thinking it was pretty cool though. It's so good to know that "No Fear" has received some attention. My guitarist, Craig Young, is nominated for musician of the year as well. I've already received some very generous birthday gifts from some people at the shows…I have the greatest fans on earth no doubt. At the end of this week, I will have played 11 shows in 12 days. It's probably more shows in that short a time than I've ever done…It's hard on the voice, but when I get out there, the smiles make me forget any fatigue.

It's time to go walk Oscar…he was constipated yesterday and he's getting that "look" in his eyes.

# August 13, 2001

I'm in Boulder, Colorado right now, and it's probably one of the most beautiful towns I've ever been to…lucky are the folks who live HERE. Now that my court date is officially over, there's something I really feel the need to say. The media has blown this situation WAY out of proportion from the the very beginning. I know there should be no need for me to defend myself in this matter, however I do want my fans to know that I have always been a very responsible drinker, and when it comes to driving while under the influence, I do not, nor have I ever, driven while impaired. When people read the officer's report about glassy eyes, they don't know that the reason was that I was up at 5:30 a.m. that morning doing radio satellite interviews (20+ stations) and was EXHAUSTED by 11 p.m. that night. And my being talkative is NOTHING different for me, I'm always that way, it's just my personality…those who have been to my shows know that I talk too much. I was speeding the night I was pulled over, and that is why I was fined for reckless driving, as opposed to DUI. Yes, I had two to three glasses of wine with dinner, but want everyone to know, I would never have driven drunk or impaired. The reason I didn't take this case to trial is because I wanted it to be OVER. We had plenty of evidence stacked up in my favor, but I was not up for a trial. It's too emotionally draining. I have always done public service announcements against drunk driving and find it repulsive and sad that so many lives have been lost over it. Anyone will tell you not to blow into a breathalyzer, no matter how little you've had, due to their constant inaccuracy. The reason my license was restricted is not because I was driving like an idiot, but because it's a law in Tennessee when you refuse the breathalyzer (this is called the "Applied Consent Law"). My license has not been sus-pended for a year. In actuality, I will have a restricted license for 9 months, which will allow me to drive to and from anything pertaining to business. I am saddened that the media has painted me as some drunk, when in reality I've always been the one taking people's keys and hiding them so they couldn't leave my house after drinking. People will believe what they want, but I am telling my fans (the ones I really care about) the 100% TRUTH…take it or leave it. In closing, as I said before, I do NOT condone drinking and driving, and will NEVER drink even a drop and drive again…It just isn't worth it, and I hope you all follow suit. That is the last I will say about this, but wanted a chance to speak MY truth. Now, on to better subjects.

"Getting There" is moving up the charts and all those requests will certainly help the cause. We will be really busy this year, and I'm having a blast seeing everyone at the shows, as always, I have the best fans in the world. Keep on keepin' on…with NO FEAR!!!!

August 23, 2001

Egads I am just about on my last leg. Whew! What a busy summer we've had. Now I can buy Oscar that expensive food he likes so much...he's such a prima donna. I just saw the new Country Weekly issue, with my tattoo picture...I did my own makeup for that shot, and I must say, I think I did a pretty darn good job on it too. We have our old drummer, Chuck, joining back up with us tomorrow, so we had a little impromptu rehearsal at my house yesterday. Think we woke up the neighbors for sure. I'm getting ready for the CCMA show...I've been working out a lot lately and estimate I've lost close to 15 lbs. I really needed to shed my winter coat, as it's miserable playing the dusty, sweaty fair circuit feeling like a sausage stuffed into a pair of jeans. The documentary that was shot in the spring is getting ready to air on CMT Canada (Terri Clark "REAL"). This is a pretty personal look at my life and I hope that people like the way it turned out. I think the film company did a very nice job indeed.

I found out I've been invited to the men's

Olympic Canadian hockey team dinner in Calgary on Sept. 6th...I'm pretty jazzed about that, as Wayne Gretzky and all the pros will be there. I don't know that much about hockey, but I know it's an opportunity I would not want to miss. I'll get an opportunity to see my grandparents and catch up with some friends, as well as do all the stuff surrounding country music week in Canada, so it should be a really fun trip. We're getting all the details for the headline tour in Canada in Nov. ironed out as we speak, and it looks like it will be a really cool month. "Getting There" is taking so long on the American charts, that we still haven't solidified a video plan yet. It is however at #8 in Canada, so all is well in the homeland. It looks like I may be working with a new producer on some of the songs on the next album, so I guess music and life itself is ever-changing. I think as an artist, growth and experimentation are necessary to keep everything fresh and new. I'm looking forward to writing a lot in October, and already have a few songs in the can. I've heard recently that I will be going to Australia in January...boy, now that will be exciting! I've never been off this continent, what with juggling Canada and the US, it's been all I could do to keep working those two countries, and I'm very delighted at the prospect of trying to break through in another market. Maybe I will try to wrestle a crocodile...NOT!!!!

September 2, 2001

Well, we've been having a great time this weekend in Canada. The show in Sunderland, Ontario was just WILD. I felt like Garth Brooks for a second there. The show in Brome, Quebec was the first sellout crowd the fair has had in 83 years...it did my ol' heart good to hear that. We were in the Eastern Townships of Quebec, and it was some of the most gorgeous land I've ever seen. I went for walks in the country and ran into a herd of cows. They just stood there staring at me, then followed me as far as they could till the fence ended. I looked at them and said, "You better watch it girls, I'm on a protein diet!" The show in Brome was interesting cause they had a whole week of acts that were "tribute" shows. Monday they have "Shania Twain," and Tuesday they have a girl doing a "tribute" to Britney Spears...I got up there and asked the audience "Why, with all the impersonators here this week, how can you be so sure I AM Terri Clark?" I think I scared them for a second...they probably thought they got ripped off!

The CCMA's are coming up soon…I'm looking forward to it. I'll get to see some family, as well as my friends in the biz in Canada. The documentary is airing in Canada tonight as well. I only wish there was some way that my American friends could see it too…maybe someday. I've had some road personnel changes this week. Greg Kaczor is coming back into the band as our acoustic player…Robby Vaughn left for personal reasons, and Greg decided he wanted to step down from road manager to play in the band again. Greg has always done a great job for me, no matter which role he's played and we're all thrilled to have him back in the band with us.

On a different note, "Getting There" is not getting there. It's done great north of the border (it's going top-5 next week), but in the US there just wasn't enough enthusiasm from radio pro-grammers and consultants to make it happen. I guess this is all part of the career ups and downs, and I try to look at the bright side of things. I'm going into the studio in October with a new producer to try a few things out, thus we begin the process again. There may be another single or two in Canada, but it doesn't look like much else will come off this album in the US. When I look at people who've had careers that span 10-20 years, they don't all have albums that commercially blow out the win-dows…however, I am, and will forever be, proud of *Fearless* and thankful to my record label for allowing me to spread my wings creatively and do the album the way I wanted to. I got so many letters and so much support from people who love it (artists, critics and fans alike), and I believe it helped so many in a positive way, and THAT is what music is all about...Before this turns into a book...time to go shower, shave the legs, and walk the dog...oh yeah, and go sing for the crowd in Walkerton, Ontario!!!!

 # September 11, 2001

I don't really know where to start here. I'm sitting at my mom's computer in Edmonton absolutely at a loss for words. This has been the most tragic day in American history that I can ever remember. Last night was a joyful celebration, and so much love was shared at the CCMA show in Calgary, and then we woke up this morning to the news about terrorist attacks on the US. It's unbelievable how much can change in a matter of moments. Last night was such a heartwarming, wonderful night for me, and I was flattered to see some American fans attending the show to cheer me on...however now I feel terrible reading that someone is stranded away from family en route back home from the show because of this mess. My heart and soul goes out to all the victims and family members of this horrendous act. I, like many others, am glued to the television, and can't fly anywhere, as all the airports are shut down. I know the London show is cancelled, and I'm still not sure about the weekend shows. At least I'm safe and with family. This hits pretty close to home, in light of the fact that I've spent so much time in New York this summer, and even played a show between the Twin Towers in July…I'm sure some of the business folks who came out to listen on their lunch breaks, we may have lost today. At times when it's an embarrassment to be a human being, we must remember all of those who are giving blood and doing all they can to help, and realize that most of the people in this world are still good. God bless everyone.

# September 17, 2001

Well, let's see…where did I leave off? Last time I wrote I was in Canada at my mother's. On Friday, Jeff Ross, Greg, Craig and I were on our way out the door rushing to the Edmonton airport to try and catch a flight to Toronto that we had been told was cancelled, which turned out not to be true (does this make any sense at all?). ANYWAY—en route to the airport, my business manager calls from Nashville and informs me that there is a charter Lear jet ready and fuelled in Nashville with all the credentials to get over the border to retrieve us. When I heard the price of the trip, I nearly choked on my breakfast…I have a very nice record label prez, who told me he would help me out with half of it…sooooooo, we turn around and go back to mom's to wait for the jet to get to Edmonton. I think Craig nearly had a heart attack when he saw the size of the plane; he's never been on one that small. I flew in one similar, one night while on tour with Reba McEntire, and she let me ride home on her plane after a show…so I knew they were FAST.

This thing was a 6-seater and got us to Nashville in 3 and a half hours...home by Friday at 10 p.m. We were able to reschedule the Saturday show in Winston-Salem for December and we made it home in time for the show on Sunday. I think we all needed to be happy for that hour and a half. I was scheduled to do a 60 minute show, but when I heard about all the fans driving from all over to get there, I asked if I could play longer, and the fair said I could. It felt good to be able to at least contribute to the healing of this country by seeing people smile and sing along. Sometimes I forget what a gift music is, and how lucky I am to get to make a living making people happy...times like this really bring that home. We had the American Flag hanging as the backdrop, and although I could feel the sadness, I could also feel the pride in that room. I had many fans show up to congratulate me on the Fan's Choice Award, and it was a great feeling. I found out today that a bunch of artists who were in Calgary last Wednesday did a benefit show at the Jubilee auditorium. What a wonderful way to try and help the victims of these attacks. I missed out, because I wasn't in the city, and wish I'd known, because I would have been there, without a doubt. I have a couple of days off now and am taking care of business, then back out on the road this weekend...The Canadian tour is coming along very nicely. It looks like we'll have Jason McCoy in most markets, as well as Gary Allan in the east…am I a lucky girl or WHAT?!

September 27, 2001

Well, I've had such a nice few days off. I went to write with my ol' pal Tom Shapiro yesterday...one of those "don't mess with me buddy" songs...gotta love 'em. Went to a birthday party that was a blast...we all sat around pickin' and singing everything from Gordon Lightfoot to Bill Monroe. It's funny how we all do this music thing for a living, but still can't get enough. The tickets have gone on sale for the first leg of the Canadian tour, and the first day was a big success...looks like we'll have a ball there in November. I'm going to Toronto in October to shoot a video for "Empty." The song will be released to country and adult contemporary radio in Canada at the end of October. The video will only be seen on CMT Canada, as it's only a Canadian release. I'm so happy the song is getting its shot somewhere, as I feel it's the strongest ballad I've written. I'm currently starting to wrap my head around the next album. I have found, and written, a couple of things, and we plan on starting it in December. I don't anticipate it will take an enormous amount of time to complete, but I need to be sure we have exactly what we need to kick things back into gear. I'll be doing some work with Byron Gallimore (Tim McGraw, Jo Dee Messina, Faith Hill), who has a pretty strong track record, so I hope it goes as well as we anticipate. I will forever feel that *Fearless* was an album that I poured my heart and soul into, and will always take pride in what I did, no matter what the charts or sales numbers said. My grassroots following has grown, and the fans have gotten everything out of it that I put into it, and that's what really counts in the end. I'm starting to feel that I'm getting a sense of "normalcy" back after the tragedy in NYC. It's something that has forever changed me and society as a whole, but I'm starting to finally sleep a bit better again. Looking forward to the shows this weekend and playing Billy Bob's again…we always have a good turnout and the crowd rocks…love those ones! Until next time…

October 3, 2001

I've had a nice few days off this week, enjoying time with my niece and grandmother. I actually zipped into the chatroom on my website the other night, which is something I don't do too often. I guess the danger of the Internet is that people can misconstrue your feelings a bit. I get the impression people feel like I'm down or unhappy, which is certainly not the case. I also heard a ridiculous rumor that I am leaving Mercury records, which is SO not the case. Never before has my label been as supportive as they are right now and I'm lucky to be there. I'm in the middle of yet another management change, but that is the only thing that's different. I'm looking forward to playing in Oklahoma again this weekend, as it's been awhile. I guess it's Tulsa time. Oscar needs a bath again...I've never seen a dog who needs deodorant more than this one...stinky armpits on a dog? I am NOT kidding, it's the strangest thing.

October 24, 2001

It's been a long time since I've had time to do a journal entry. I've been writing new songs, looking for songs, and getting ready for the Big Canadian tour, and I must say, I think I needed to get out on the road to get some REST!!! It's been quite an interesting month to say the least. I'm keeping up with the current events of the War on Terrorism and all the anthrax scares, however, I try not to glue myself to the news. I really don't feel fear about any of this. I feel that the statistics show we have a better chance of being struck by lightning than being a victim of a terrorist attack, however it's sad to see that they are successful in throwing the entire nation into a panic (which is what they really want to achieve). Anyway, enough about that...

We left Nashville on Monday night and just arrived in Price, Utah. It turned really cold and windy somewhere along the way within 2 hours, and it was hard for the driver to keep it between the lines for a bit of the trip. We stopped in Cheyenne for dinner, then drove all night. I spent most of yesterday in my bunk listening to a big bag of songs that have been pitched to me for my next album. It's a very tedious and difficult process, but I've found a few really good ones. The tour should be really neat. We're carrying more production that I ever have before...a few cool surprises during the show and we're reworking "When Boy Meets Girl," which should come as a shock to some when they hear what we're doing to it. We shoot the video for "Empty" in Edmonton on November 6th...I have designed a really cool shirt that someone is making for me to wear. The video concept will strictly be me performing the song in a neat theater setting...no kissy-face, over-the-top, lovey-dovey stuff...been there, done that...I like the simple approach much better for this particular song. I'm glad we're releasing that song in Canada; it really deserves a shot somewhere. We're going to send a separate mix to the AC stations as well, so I may get air-play in some places that don't have a country station.

We stopped at Wal-Mart in Cheyenne last night and I got a striped sweater for Oscar. Then I found a little hat that looked like the top of a pumpkin that you tie on the dog's head... needless to say, Oscar was NOT amused, however we laughed our butts off, and took some hysterical pictures. Speaking of pictures...a fan sent me a disposable camera to take pictures with, so I did (in Anderson) from the stage, and on the bus...and sent it back to her...some of the pictures were pretty stupid, but I wonder if she got a laugh out of them? I think I took a picture of someone's behind, and some of the dog, and some of really dumb things like fast food restaurants, and a cracker on the floor, the bus toilet...I am weird.

November 10, 2001

Well, this is going to be a quick one today. We've been pretty busy these days with the Canadian tour. I must say I'm having a total blast up here, and the reviews have been awesome. We're going to post some on the website. We shot the video for "Empty" in Edmonton last week. I think it's going to look really nice. I hardly wore the cowboy hat at all in this one. We all felt the song was a very soft intimate vibe, and that it wouldn't have been as appropriate. They're hoping it will air sometime around the 15th on CMT Canada. I'm hearing tell of a petition to get the song released in the US...I'm so flattered that my fans would go to that kind of trouble. I'm not sure what the result will be, however, I'm grateful for the effort. I've heard that the song is being added to some E-Z Rock stations in Canada as well as Country, so I'm glad it will have an even broader audience than my other singles have.

My mom cooked dinner for the whole band on the 7th, while we were in Edmonton. We watched part of the CMA show...I couldn't go due to the Canadian schedule, however I was invited to present...oh well...It would've killed me to fly all the way back to Nashville, then back to Alberta in less than 24 hours as we had a show on the 8th in a remote area. Mom had everyone over to the digs for a home-cooked meal (something we could all use by now). We had a grand time at the Clarks. I also got to go see a movie at the mall, and shop at the Roots clothing store...gotta love it! The guys and me have all been trying to fight off colds and sickness at one time or another...as soon as one feels better, someone else gets it...GEEZ! We're going through echinacea and vitamin C like crazy. We're in Fort McMurray today...It's FREEZING!!!!!!!

November 23, 2001

Well, here I am at home (it's hard to believe it!!!) eating leftover turkey...yum yum-mmm. I honestly think I prefer leftovers to the real deal...there's something about reheated stuff that just rocks my world...I really like left-over macaroni and cheese too (Kraft Dinner to us Canucks). My mom is down in Nashville for a couple of weeks, visiting and helping me out with some business affairs. We've had my two nieces here for the week, so needless to say it's been quite eventful. I realize now that at 7 a.m. the phrase "The pitter-patter of tiny feet" is totally non-existent in the REAL world. They sounded more like baby elephants crashing into walls over and over again...I love them so, but GEEZ, it was hard to sleep in. I'm on the road schedule...which means 1-2 a.m. to bed, 10 a.m. to rise...NOT GOOD! We took the girls to the matinee show of *Harry Potter* today...it was a looooong movie, but they were mesmerized throughout...as was I. I read the first two books about a year ago, and had been anticipating the release of the movie. I'm such a kid at heart. I think I was first in line to buy the *Shrek* DVD when it came out. We watched that yesterday (Thanksgiving)…after we ate our third plate of turkey dinner. I'm always in charge of the mashed potatoes…even though they end up all over the place…I guess that's what happens when you use the electric mixer and forget to turn it off when you take it out of the bowl!!! I hired a new manager this past week—Clarence Spalding with TBA in Nashville. He's been in the Brooks and Dunn camp for many years and we really clicked…I'm very excited about the future and working with him. I go into the studio Dec. 10th to cut 2-3 things for the next album with Byron Gallimore. We have found a couple of songs we both like, and are going to see how we "click" musically. Tommorow it's back on the bus time at 2 p.m…going to the Eastern part of Canada for the rest of the tour. I'm going to try and get some Christmas shopping done while I'm there, since the dollar is so low in Canada…that benefits those of us with US funds…Well, I guess I should go to bed now…7 a.m. comes pretty early around here.

December 7, 2001

Well, here I am back home again safe and sound, after a very loooooong time on the road. We have two more shows left for the year, then a nice little break. My guitar player, Craig, won't be with us for the show in N.C. this weekend, so Kevin and I get to swap lead guitar duties (mostly Kevin—thank God). I had a great time in Toronto the past three days, visiting with my sister and nephew. My mom also happened to be visiting at the same time, so we all had a blast together. My sister and I got to go out one night for a "girls night out," and had the best time. We had dinner and saw the movie *K-Pax*...then went to a place not far from her house. We met a guy named Kyle, who came up to our table 5 minutes after we walked in, and said "I'm having an episode over here." I looked over and saw about 5 people all staring in my direction. He told us that a group of people bet him that I was Terri Clark, and he had bet that I wasn't. Well, I told him my name was Tracy and had him going for over half an hour. He was convinced I was a barrel racer from

Calgary. I didn't want him to lose the bet, 'cause he bet money, and was funny and nice, so we waited till the other people left, and then what happened next was hysterically funny. We were all talking, and he was engaged in deep conversation with my sister, when I found one of my signature guitar picks in my coat pocket (I usually never have these on me). I just put it on the table in front of him, waiting for him to notice it. When he did, his face was priceless... mouth gaping open, the whole nine yards (with a few cuss words thrown in)...I wish I'd had a camera for that one. Anyway, he was just so funny, and we all ended up having a great time...I even got up to sing a few songs...just can't keep me away from the stage I guess, even on a day off. I'm so excited about putting up my Christmas tree this year and being domestic for awhile...Gee, I guess it really is the simple things in life that matter, right?...Even for a girl named "Tracy. "

Terri

P.S. We played 3 songs for the Sports Network in Toronto, at the Special Olympics fundraiser dinner on Wednesday night. It was a formal gala with a lot of people dressed to the nines. I met Judd Nelson (the actor), and had all of these flashbacks to my teenage years, and movies like *The Breakfast Club*, and *St. Elmo's Fire*...WHEW.

The tour jacket promo we did on the Canadian tour with radio stations raised a total of $13,576 for The Special Olympics. The president of The Special Olympics told me that money would send 10 athletes to Ireland for the World games next year; now THAT feels good!!!

December 25, 2001

It's December 25th...Christmas Day. I'm sitting here, so full from turkey dinner, I can't move. I got a lot of nice things this year. The thing I cherish the most is time spent with family, real personal, normal time. It seems that I see a lot of family during my Canadian tours, and I always regret that there is so much hustle and bustle going on, that we have no quality time...that is what Christmas is for. My little brother and I opened one present on Christmas Eve. I got a new toothbrush holder and soap dish. He got a three year subscription to *Roughneck Magazine*. He's a 20-year-old oil rig worker and seemed very excited about it...I was laughing my $#@ off...I just never imagined there could even be a *Roughneck Magazine*. I'm going to a ski hill with mom tomorrow...I hope it's like riding a bike...it's been a few years. I went to the big West Edmonton Mall the other day to do some last minute shopping...I tried to get everyone what they needed, my mother is always good at tipping me off as to who needs what...mothers just know these things. We had my stepfather's mother over for Christmas Eve, and Christmas Day dinner. She is 90 years old...and really neat to talk to. We got into a conversation about the Beatles at dinner...she remembered the first time she heard of them (she is from Britian)...all I could do was sit there and think to myself, She was 55 years old when the Beatles were introduced to the public...WOW! That seems like forever ago, but it really wasn't to her...it's all relative I guess.

On Dec. 10th we recorded three songs for the next album. They're all uptempo, really great songs...none of which I wrote...I'm writing my butt off all of January, and we'll cut more of those the end of February...I'm really excited about working with Byron Gallimore...we hit it off the first go round, so I'm relaxed about the rest of it. The apple pie has just arrived from the oven...gotta go...

January 9, 2002

Here we are…2002. Well, I guess this marks the anniversary of the first year of my journal. I've been really busy writing songs, doing demos, recording the new album, and trying to have a life in between. New Year's Eve I was in bed by 11:30, and fell asleep before midnight…I guess skiing will do that to you…either that, or I'm just plain GETTING OLD! It was nice to get back to Tennessee after Christmas. The temperature where I was most of the holidays were dipping down pretty low, and I had a perpetual wad of Kleenex stuck up my nose the entire time. I went to Tootsie's the other night and had a grand time…saw a bunch of folks I hadn't seen in quite awhile. This time of year always tends to be very reflective for me, hence, very conducive to songwriting as well. The holidays were so great, but also very quiet this year. After the hectic touring schedule and events of last year, that was just FINE with me!!!! Nothing is more exciting to me than lying around the house in sweatpants, in front of the fire, with…er, gravy all over my shirt. Well, I'm

going to write another song here in a few minutes, so I'd better get out of my flannels and put
some real clothes on.

January 17, 2002

My brain is fried…I cannot listen to anymore music with lyrics today. I have written 4 songs since last Monday, and it's time to give my wee little mind a rest…so I'm listening to Keith Jarrett…a fine mod-classical pianist as I write this. Rick Reith (my old monitor engineer) is downstairs disassembling my home studio. He's going to auction everything off on eBay for me. It's hard to see all this stuff go, since I recorded *Fearless* on it, but I just don't need it for this current album, and it's taking up a lot of room. We're doing the new record in the "new-fangled fashion" with a LARGE band down on Music Row. Ah, well sometimes you just have to say goodbye to the one you love!…besides, I'm an idiot when it comes to technology anyway!!!!! It's so neat starting a new album…hard to believe it's #5. I can imagine how people feel when they have 5 kids…well…okay not quite the same I guess…I'm enjoying being down in and amongst the songwriters here in Nashville…I've done some co-writing with Leslie Satcher, Victoria Shaw, and my old pal

Tom Shapiro wrote with Kevin Post and I today. It's great to be sitting in a room and hear Vince Gill in the next room writing a song...now THAT is cool. The Opry was a blast last weekend...my nerves were shot, as usual (they always are at the Ryman)...but I was told I didn't flub it up too badly. I got to mingle with some fans at Tootsie's for awhile afterward...My friend Tonda had a VERY good time. A bunch of guys in the band and some of my pals, all took off to another destination about midnight...it was so smoky and crowded, I was beginning to develop smoker's induced asthma...and I don't smoke! Well, I guess I'd better go and make sure Rick doesn't need any help with his...er tools...

January 24, 2002

I have a day off today...I'm not writing, however I have managed to pick up some nasty cold germ along the way somewhere, so I'll spend the day drinking OJ and watching TV. I've co-written 7 songs in the past two and a half weeks...that's a lot for me, since I usually don't write until I have a record to do...there just isn't much time during touring season. We've found some really great songs by other writers as well, so I feel like some of the pressure has been lifted as far as expectations to write a lot of the album. As of right now, I think I'll be happy if I have 4 songs on it. I found Byron Gallimore the first half. That should make for a cool mix. Keith and I have had a lot of success in the past, so it's something I'm really optimistic about...and Byron's track record speaks for itself...he IS country radio right now. Just about every song they play, he has produced!!

I'm taking a week off from it all to go and visit my grandmother. Since my Grandad passed on last year, she's been alone, so I want to take advantage of the "off-season" to go and spend a few days with her. I can't imagine being with someone for 53 years, and all of a sudden they're gone...I'm sure it's unbearable at times...

The band is gearing back up for a few shows in February. We haven't done anything since early December, so hopefully we won't hit too many clams...I have so many new song lyrics floating around in my head, I hope I remember the words to the old ones!!! We'll keep the show as was last year until the album is finished, and then we can add some new things to the show in May/June...that will be something to really look forward to...we love learning new stuff, it keeps us all "feeling fresh"...so to speak...Oscar has some serious gasses leaking out of his butt right now, so I must go and walk him...

January 31, 2002

I FINALLY got home from visiting my grandmother and her two sisters, Ida and Sarah, in Ontario. We had a great time, with unseasonably good tempuratures...like spring-time, really...for the first 3 days I was there. I arrived on Sunday afternoon, and we had roast beef and pork, with potatoes and GRAVY, and apple pie for dessert. My Nanny's two sisters look exactly like her, they all have grey/white hair, and talk the same, and walk the same, and are all within about 5 years of each others' ages. They are commonly referred to as "The Golden Girls." I took some great pictures while they had their hair in curlers playing Bingo and watching Bob Barker on *The Price is Right*. My Nanny is very fond of Bob...she likes him with his hair the natural color, rather than brown. She says it looks better when a person ages so that "The face matches the hair...dear." We just had the best time. I ate more food than any human should ever consume in a four day period...reminded me of the scene in the Jim Carrey movie *The Grinch*, when they were all stuffing his face with Who pudding…yes, it was much like that…but did I mind? Noooooooo.

I went out on the town Monday night with one of my best friends from WAY back…we ended up at a bar, and of course, I ended up with the entertainer's guitar singing a bunch of songs by various artists, including my own…a good time was had by all. I think "The Golden Girls" were up all night wondering what the hell I was doing out so late. The news started preparing us for a storm watch yesterday afternoon, and then, lo and behold, last night the airport called and informed me my flight to Nashville via Detroit this morning had been cancelled…I was pretty stressed, wondering how to get back to Nashville in time for Friday morning and work on the album. A big winter storm was on its way and I had to find a way back…my ticket was a connection in Detroit, but no flights were leaving Ontario at that point. I called my Dad, who is a truck driver, who often comes through Nashville to drop his trailer in Texas…turns out he had to do that very thing today. He picked me up at Nanny's at 9 a.m. and we headed to Detroit. He informed me we would cross the bridge over the border, then we would have to find a place for me to catch a cab to the airport, and HOPEFULLY I would make my 3:20 flight…he couldn't take the truck to the airport, as there was nowhere to park it. Weather was treacherous, and driving conditions were really bad…snow and freezing rain. We made it across the border at 1:30, and saw a motel close by to stop and call a cab (we were at least 20 miles from the airport). We went into the lobby, and I figured out really fast that this was NO ordinary motel, nor was this an ordinary part of town…but we had no choice. We walked into the lobby and spoke to the woman at the front desk through a large wall of Plexiglas and a spinning carousel of condoms. I asked her if she would kindly call me a cab…she said she needed a $5 deposit, then when the cab came she would give it back. She said they only dealt with ONE cab company… she called twice and nobody answered the phone. I asked her for a phone book and called a different cab company. I successfully got through and she gave me back my $5. I was short on cash and saw no ATM in sight, so I asked my Dad if I could borrow $20 when the cab arrived. When the cab pulled up to the hotel, I opened the door, and there sat a skinny, elderly African-American man with a some-what toothless smile. I asked how much it would cost for a ride to the airport…he said less than $30…My Dad handed me $20, hugged me goodbye, and sent me on my way. As soon as the door closed, the dialogue went as follows:

Driver: "You're worth more than twenty bucks!!!!"

Me: "First off, that was my father, and secondly, I am not a prostitute!" (This is particularly odd since I was in cargo pants, a T-shirt and ZERO makeup, carrying only a backpack.) "Besides, he would be too old for me anyway."

Driver: "Oh, I know what you like baby, those young ones who will just shut-up and do it right."

I won't go any further with the rest of this dialogue...this is a family show. He then proceeded to start driving (very fast) and pulled out a crumpled brown paper sack with some sort of beverage in it that resembled a beer of some kind, and finished it off. (Keep in mind, the weather is terrible, and people are in the ditches all over the place)...he says to me, "It's only one beer, just one cold beer, that's all." I say, "Don't worry, I won't tell anyone." (I wanted to get there alive). I actually arrived in one piece, after driving in a semi-tractor-trailer for 4 hours, in life-threatening conditions, being mistaken for a hooker, my Dad being mistaken for my John, and a tanked cab driver going 100 mph.

How was your day?

Tootsie's Orchid Lounge, Nashville, TN, January 22, 2003
Photographer: Eric England

 # February 20, 2002

WHEW!

I think I need to get back on the road so I can get some rest!

I've been sooooo busy lately, working on demos, and yesterday we cut three more songs for the album, plus all the writing, but I do love it so...I won't complain (too much). I've been reading people's posts about being anxious for the new album. We still have a lot more to do, but from the direction it seems to be taking, it's hard to describe exactly what it's like, but I would say definitely rockin' kick-ass country... I've taken a lot of the pressure off myself to write all of these songs, therefore I'm cutting a lot of songs that Nashville songwriters have contributed. I may only have 3-4 of my own on there, but they will be ones that come straight from the heart. I think I've found that I didn't want to start repeating myself with songs I write, and after 6 years of it, I was feeling like the uptempo ideas were wearing a bit thin, so I'm relaxing a bit and writing what comes from the heart, and cutting other people's songs that aim for radio and the mainstream...that way I get the best of both worlds...works for me!

Byron Gallimore has been a real treat to work with and I'm happy to say *Billboard Magazine* has awarded him 2001's HOT Country Producer...I would say he certainly deserves it. I'm doing the second half of the album with Keith Stegall and we'll be doing some of my own songs, as well as a couple of really traditional country-sounding things...ain't nothin' like a real good country song...I'm hoping for a later fall album release, with the single coming this summer, but we'll see how the scheduling shakes down at the record label before it's set in stone. Well, gotta run...going to write today...

February 22, 2002

WE GOT THE GOLD
WE GOT THE GOLD
WE GOT THE GOOOOOOOOOOLD!!!!!!!!!!!!!!

I have a few friends on the Canadian Women's Olympic Hockey team, and I'm so happy for them. This means so much to the team and will give them opportunities they've not been able to have in the past...HOORAY! I'm sending a congrats note and a slew of *Fearless* ball caps their way ASAP. I went to a party for Byron Gallimore yesterday. He has been named *Billboard Magazine*'s Producer of the Year for the third year in a row, so they threw a big par-tay for him...it was a surprise too. I don't know how they kept it from him, since EVERYONE in the music industry was there, including Tim, Faith, Martina, Phil Vassar, Jessica Andrews, yours truly, and most of Music Row. The aforementioned artists all brought their children, who all happen to be little girls under the age of seven, so one corner of the room was occupied by the pitter-patter of tiny feet…it was so cute and nice to see everyone.

Well…I just wanted to gloat about the gold medal a bit and drop some names!!!!!!!! Time to go mix my demo session…

February 24, 2002

GOLD GOLD GOOOOOOOOOLD!!!!!! I watched the game today, and must say, once again was jumping up and down. Team Canada got the Olympic gold for the first time in 50 years. I went to the Team Canada dinner in Calgary the week before the CCMA's in September. I took my cousin Steven with me (who is a hockey fanatic). We hung out with all the players from the Men's and Women's teams. I don't think Steven expected to even meet Wayne Gretzky or Mario Lemieux, but when Gretzky asked if we wanted to eat dinner at their table, he almost passed out…(I thought it was pretty cool too). A table of six, and there we were. The guys were so kind to Steven and I, and we spent a few quality hours sitting and talking with the greatest hockey players in the world. They gave me a box full of Team Canada jerseys, sweatshirts and T-shirts, so needless to say I wore my jersey all day today…what a JOY!

March 10, 2002

I just finished watching the 9-11 documentary on CBS. It is so surreal that something like this could actually have happened. It's hard to comprehend that the buildings I played between on July 26th are gone, as well as so many of the people of New York City along with them. I remember looking at the fountain while we played on the stage that was attached to the North Tower. I remember looking at the people coming out of the Towers for their lunch break to watch the Country show that was going on. I signed autographs for some of those people. A friend of mine recently put together a beautiful display containing 3 pictures of the show that day, with the backstage "All Access" pass that Greg Kaczor still had, and framed all of it for me. It's just something for me to look at and remember what it was like before the world changed. I remember struggling with whether or not to play that show, because the schedule was so jammed last summer...now I'm so glad I did. We spent so much time in NYC this past summer, after the show at the Trade Center we all walked the streets that afternoon, going to stores and "McSorley's," an ancient trademark pub that has been there for over a hundred years. I guess this documentary made me reminisce about a different, better time. I was really sick all last week with a throat infection. I can't remember being that sick in years. I'm a person who has a pretty sturdy immune system, but I think the schedule I've been keeping the past few weeks just put me down for a while. I watched a lot of movies and ate a lot of soup, 'cause it hurt too much to swallow anything else. The album is coming along very nicely, and everyone is excited about getting it in the can and out there for the radio folks to hear. I think we have a great mix of songs that everyone can relate to…including myself, of course. Anyway…will write more later, but it's my bedtime now.

March 26, 2002

Here comes Peter Cottontail...hopping down the bunny trail...hippity, hoppity... Easter's on its WAY!!!!! I love Easter...mostly because I get presents from my Mommy...back when I was a kid it was lots of chocolate, but she knows I have a photo shoot coming up, so I think she'll be sending me underwear or something like that this year.

Had a groovy time in Florida last week. I bought a new summer wardrobe and things I can wear during fair season...nice Caribbean-type shirts with little fish and birds on them. I kinda look like Magnum P.I. minus all the facial hair. Been writing my brains out for the record. We go in on April 8th-9th to cut the second half, so we're honing in on the remainder of the songs we're going to do. I have demo sessions next week and last minute meetings to make final decisions. The band is working up a couple of new songs to play for our gigs in April, one being Billy Bob's, which is always a fun time. It's rainy and cold outside today, so I think I will stay in and take care of some business...maybe write a song about rain…like that's never been done before! I watched myself on *Diagnosis Murder* last night…actually I was FORCED to watch it by my friends…embarrassing…to say the least. Hollywood's take on the country music industry is hysterical…stereotypical as can be. My acting could use a little work…God my hair was looooong back then…and my a*# was small. Oh well…*que sera sera*!

April 17, 2002

Well, I guess it's about time for an update. I've been working feverishly at finishing as much of the album as I can before venturing off to the CMT Spring Fling in Barbados. I know that it will be a work-related vacation, but I can certainly use a few days on the beach. We cut 6 sides with Keith Stegall last week, and they sound great. Byron and Keith have recorded 5 songs that I've co-written, and 6 songs that were written by songwriters in the Nashville community. It's a very eclectic group of songs that range from pure country to country rock. It's an album I feel like we'll all be proud of, and I'm so looking forward to getting it out there for public consumption.

We played three shows in Texas last weekend. It's so much fun to get back to playing live after being in the studio so much, but certainly takes some readjustment. I get out of that "mode" and it's hard to flip the switch on and off when we only have three shows in 6 weeks. I'm grateful for the wonderful response we got at Billy Bob's last Saturday night. It was probably the most enthusiastic, energized crowd I've ever played to in that venue…I'm also thrilled at the response that "I Just Wanna Be Mad" has been getting when I play it live…it's always great to run new material by the fans first. I have to head back to the studio in a few minutes…better get some lunch and let Oscar out…

May 2, 2002

Well, all I have to say is I now have a FABUTAN!!!!!! Barbados was so much fun and very relaxing, at a time I could certainly use it. The fans who won the trips were very sweet and respectful of the artists' privacy the whole time. We were all at the same resort, but I didn't even know who they were until we had our Pottery Class. I made a replica of Oscar doing his sitting-up trick, and an ashtray for my pal Tonda who complains that I don't ever have one when she comes to visit...this one has her name on it, so she can't miss it. I had a nice time visiting with my friends Mark Wills and Chely Wright as well...a good time was had by all. We got right back to work on the album upon my return to Nashville. Vince Gill was kind enough to come in yesterday and lend his vocals on a song I wrote with Rory Lee called "Better Than You"...it's RRRREEEEEEALY country and he sounded fantastic singing on it. The last time Vince and I sang together was on a demo project I did in 1992 before I had a record deal...I was so happy that now it's for real and everyone can hear it. I'm gearing up for the photo shoot in Los Angeles next week (yes, I am STARVING for a french fry). We're going to be shooting in a gorgeous location, and the clothing stylist has some neat, fresh ideas...one of which is me wearing...um...a thong!...Just kidding! We're gearing up for the summer touring season as well. Greg will be going back to tour manager duties the first of June, and we'll have a brand new face behind the acoustic guitar, as well as a new guy playing fiddle. I'm excited to get a fiddle back in the band...it was necessary due to all the fiddle parts on the new album. Time to go and eat some raw carrots...NOT!!!!

May 30, 2002

Well, it's been a whirlwind for the past three weeks. After the Barbados Spring Fling, I flew to Los Angeles where we did the latest photo shoot for the album artwork. We shot pictures at an old hotel in Palm Springs called Balentines. Then went out to Joshua Tree National Park the second day to shoot outside. It was so windy I was barely able to keep my hat on! After getting home from the shoot, Greg and I flew to Washington DC for an autograph session for WMZQ. The next day, my friend (and bass player) Jeff and I caught a flight to Europe. I've never been to Europe and decided I would take the opportunity to do some travelling abroad as my vacation time before we get full swing into promoting the new album and single. We did it the ol'-fashioned way, on trains, planes and automobiles. We were able to hit England, France, Italy and the French Riviera. Jeff took a bunch of great black-and-white photos, which he will hand tint (that's his other job). I was so awestruck with the beauty, history and architecture, that all I was able to do was snap a bunch of pictures and gawk like the tourist I was. He's travelled Europe many times, and it was so nice to have a built-in tour guide who knew what he was doing and where he was going! I've arrived safely back in Nashville, and am gearing up for June touring, and finishing up the album…It's going to be a very busy time for me in the next few months, so I'm enjoying the calm before the storm…so to speak!

June 18, 2002

Another year goes by, and with that, another fan club party. I don't know why, but every year seems to be an improvement on the last one. I did an acoustic solo music program this year, with some accompaniment by Craig, and we had a ball...of course I forgot a lot of the proper chord progressions, but don't think anyone minded. Everyone was soooo nice and generous with their kind words and thoughtful gifts. I'm a very blessed person to have the kind of fans I do, who appreciate what I do, even in between albums...speaking of which...It's looking like we'll have a late summer single release date and the album will be out in the new year. We're all very excited about this album and have spent a lot of time working on it to get it as right as we can. It was fun playing a few new songs at the party yesterday and getting some good initial reactions from the folks who matter the most. I'm looking forward to playing the Opry again on Friday night as well. I guess I'll close for now and start planning next year's Fan Club Party!!!!!!

July 9, 2002

Well, it's official. "I Just Wanna Be Mad" is going to be the first single off my still-yet-untitled album. We're still working on the single release date, and as soon as I know something, I'll be sure to share the information. I haven't seen my record label this pumped in a long time and it's very exciting for all of us.

I went to Cincinnati to see a friend play a show there and ended up doing an impromptu duet! Melissa Etheridge has always been known for having people sing with her and I'm surely no comparison to the likes of Bruce Springsteen and some of the folks she's shared the stage with, but gosh it was a fun thing to do. I did the same thing in Memphis with her a few years ago and it was even more fun this time. We have some time off this month and I plan on spending that time relaxing and getting reacquainted with long-lost friends. August is filled up and we'll be busy travelling the countryside, so I'll enjoy some downtime now, while I can. It's so hot down here in the south and the humidity is about to drive me nuts. I'm definitely a spring/fall/winter person. Although I love pool time like anyone else, the extremely hot/humid weather does not bring out the best in me...cranky, cranky, cranky!!!!

 # July 31, 2002

Well, the time is drawing nearer to the
release of "I Just Wanna Be Mad." I went to some
radio stations yesterday and we played that song,
plus 4 others from the upcoming album, and the
response was better than I could ever have hoped
for. They all told me that they were looking forward to having me back on the airwaves. We're in
Beaver Creek, Colorado today, playing on top of
a mountain. The elevation is really high, so we're
trying to watch ourselves in the altitude, as it can
make one feel short-winded and light-headed.
I'll be going to as many radio stations as I can this
month, in between all the shows we're playing,
so I won't be home more than 3-4 days this
month, but I feel it'll all be worth it in the end.
We have a new band member playing fiddle.
Her name is Janee and she's 19 years old and
very talented…I'm looking forward to everyone
hearing our new addition to the show. I'll be
shooting the video for "Mad" later this month,
possibly in Alaska, which would be really cool,
and we don't have to worry about losing daylight
either! Well, I'd better run…catering is ready!!!

August 10, 2002

EXCITED!!! That's the word to describe me right now. So many good things are happening, I just wanna scream YYYYAAAAYYYYY!!!!!

We've been visiting a lot of radio stations in between shows, and the response on "Mad" has been over-the-top positive. I was scared that the radio folks had forgotten all about me, but I was welcomed with open arms by my old friends at every station I went to, and told that this is just the song they want from me right now. They all seem to be glad to have me back, and have been generous enough to play the song early on a lot of their showdown contests at night against other songs and in the smash or trash segments. So far, I've heard we've won most of them and gotten great audience response...a good early sign. We've decided to shoot the video in San Francisco instead of Alaska...we had a last-minute idea that will require some big city lights and the vibe will be a bit more edgy, so the hay bails will have to wait. For anyone who's seen the Mitsubishi commercial with the

Barenaked Ladies song and people singing in the car with the city whizzing by…it will be more like that…a very cool concept. The same guys who did my "Poor, Poor Pitiful Me" video will be doing it (Deaton and Flannigan). We're all excited to get to work together again. I'm enjoying playing to some familiar faces and some new ones as well…the shows are always the most fun part for me…although I'm really tired from all the travel and preparation going on, it will all be worth it in the end…life is GOOD!!!!

August 19, 2002

Today has been a wonderful day. I got a call from my record label telling me that my single was the second most added (to radio playlists) in the country this week. Faith Hill was first. I can't say what a great feeling it is. "I Just Wanna Be Mad" was the Hotshot Debut in Billboard at #51 and it was a week before the actual airplay date. I hope and pray it continues to go this well. I got to thank a bunch of my fans in person in a hotel hallway this past weekend. It sure helps to have a core fan-base that supports you through the ups and downs of this crazy business. It was good to spend some time letting them know how much their loyalty means to me. I'm getting ready to do a big satellite tour tomorrow morning, starting at 6 a.m., going out all over the country to several radio stations. The next two days will be well spent travelling via satellite; it's better than having to fly everywhere! I'm getting my wardrobe together for the video shoot next weekend, and look forward to having something current on CMT and GAC again. I get to go to Alaska for the first time as well next week...I'll report back again after all the happenings of the week have passed and fill you in on all the gory details.

September 2, 2002

I figured I would catch up while I had a moment on this glorious Labor Day. I've been very busy and doing a lot of travelling lately. We went to Alaska for a show for the very first time last week. It was probably one of the most majestic places I have ever been to. I only wish we could have had a wee bit more time to see the sights. We had a sold-out crowd, so with any luck we'll get to go back again sometime. The video shoot for "I Just Wanna Be Mad" went great. We shot in various parts of San Francisco all night long until about 4 a.m. It'll be very different from anything I've done yet, and I look forward to seeing the final result at the end of the week. I was wearing my cowboy hat (which happens to be a George Strait Resistol…always) in virtually every shot for this one. The CCMA show is coming up on Monday night and I look forward to seeing all my friends in the biz again…it's a great opportunity to catch up with each other since our paths don't often cross. I'll be performing "Mad" on the show with my entire band, so it'll be great to have everyone there with me this year. The single moved up another 7 spots on the R&R chart this week from 43 to 36. I'm so excited I can't stand it...I'm glad it seems there is still a place for me in this music I love so much...having a ball as always...

September 13, 2002

My, oh my, what an exciting two weeks I've had. First I got to sing the National anthem in Baltimore at the Orioles first winning game in a losing streak. I was awarded one of the coveted collector's bobbleheads after the game, which made my day, of course. The radio station was so kind to us, and they had a stage set up before the game that we played on for 30 minutes as the crowd gathered by the front gates...what a blast. Then we headed off to Wheeling, West Virginia, for a show in the famous Capitol Theater. The response to the new songs from my upcoming album, *Pain To Kill* due Jan. 7-03, is awesome. We played "Three Mississippi" for some of the fans who had yet to hear it live, and "I Just Wanna Be Mad" is getting great response. Then off to the CCMA show in Calgary, Alberta we went. We played at the industry President's Dinner on Sunday night, and got a lot of compliments on the new material, which was what we focused on for all three songs. The Awards show was great this year, and it was so nice to see all my peers again. It was great to see my friend Paul Brandt get Album and Male Artist this year; he works very hard. I was in utter shock when I received the Fan's Choice for Entertainer of the Year. We worked a lot in Canada last year, and it was such an honor to be recognized for what we do out on the road every night. I will say it yet one more time…I have the greatest fans in the world, and they stick by me through thick and thin…Nobody can take that away!

September 27, 2002

Woke up at 5 a.m. this morning to get ready for a radio morning visit in Ft. Lauderdale, Florida. It was very early, and I knew I had to sing, so I drank 3 cups of coffee (which I don't normally drink unless needed), and I was about as amped up as I could be. I think the studio audience thought I was crazy…which isn't far from the truth really. Last week was so exciting as the song jumped 9 spaces on the Radio and Records chart…everyone on my business team jumped for joy and let out a very loud cheer that was probably heard all the way down Music Row. It's so fun to be getting a bit of a fresh start and be just as excited now as I was in 1995, just OLDER…those 5 a.m. wake-up calls are a lot harder now. I play two club shows this weekend. I must say it's nice to get a change of scenery. Inside it's a lot less muddy. The album is officially coming out January 7th. I anticipate doing a lot to promote it during the winter months, and look forward to sharing the new music with everyone. The video premieres tonight on CMT…I'm looking forward to hearing what the fans say about it. I'm going to go to the club early and watch the TV in the manager's office so I can see it. The satellite isn't working on the bus today and my hotel room doesn't have CMT. I'm sure we'll all be crowded around a tiny TV looking like a bunch of goobers.

October 12, 2002

Here I am sitting at the Hampton Inn of the day, in El Paso, Texas. We haven't been here since 1995 so we had a great, very enthusiastic crowd to play to. Someone decided to bring me her request in person and got thrown off the stage. I always feel sorry for people who get tackled when they climb up there, but I guess that's what security is there to do...I never know quite what to do except wave goodbye. We go to California for some dates tomorrow. I love the crowds and the climate out there, and always so look forward to it. The Crazy Horse is one of my favorite venues and we play there religiously once a year at least. I went to New York City this week to play privately for some media people at the Cowgirl Hall of Fame. We had ribs, slaw, and good down home cookin', and I rendered a few tunes for the city folks. They seemed very pleased with the songs I played for them, although I was fighting the crowd noise in the bar next to our private room. I just sang as loud as I could and tried hard as hell to drown them all out. We're doing the same in L.A. at the end of the month. I have the best PR I've had yet, and am very excited about the prospects. The single is doing great...spins increase every week, and we're moving up the charts nicely. All the radio folks are telling me it's going to be a big hit...feels really good to hear that. All in all, life is very good, and I enjoy seeing the fans out in the audience coming to the shows. We're working up a few new things over the next couple of days, another new song from the album and a couple of surprises. Time to go and watch what the pet psychic is up to tonight...God help me!

November 1, 2002

Well, here I am after a week long excursion to Los Angeles. I did a TV Guide Channel interview and a piece for CNN at the Guitar Center that will air around my album release time. I got to mess around and jam on all kinds of cool vintage guitars. One in particular was a 1948 Telecaster that was going for $18,000. Oh well...it was fun to dream. I plugged into a Marshall amp and turned it up so loud my fillings almost came out. The folks there were all great and I can't wait till I get to do that again. Speaking of album release, I'm now hearing it's been pushed to January 14th. "Mad" is doing so well on the charts and we're all so excited every Monday when we get the new numbers. I'll be running my butt off next week during all the CMA events taking place. I'll be doing the Opry tomorrow night. I'm fighting a bit of a scratchy throat so I can only hope I don't suck. TV always rattles me a bit, but every time I do it, the less nervous I get. I also am presenting an award on the CMA show Wednesday, as well as doing a bunch of radio stuff and photo shoot for

USA Today…it's all good stuff, but I know I'll be tired by the end of the week. We're playing a club tonight in Bartlett, Illinois…I hear it's a sold out show, so that's pretty darn cool. Hunger pains are starting to creep up on me so…

November 20, 2002

I figured I'd better do a journal entry before Thanksgiving week kicks in and I get too busy eating and forget about writing. I'll be flying to Minneapolis tomorrow night to meet the bus, then we drive into North Dakota for our show on Friday night. This has been a very busy year for me, with making a new album, as well as writing, recording demos, looking for songs, and playing about 75 dates on the road. I'm ready for some R&R time over the holidays to reflect on all my blessings and spend time with the family. We have a few more gigs before then, so I'm looking forward to playing for the people a few more times this year, and already next year is looking to be a very busy one out on the road. The success of "Mad" continues to just blow me away and it's hard to contain my excitement...we're all keeping our fingers crossed that it continues on this path. I'll be doing some more writing in December, so I'm really looking forward to that as well. Jann Arden sent me her new *Live with the Vancouver Symphony* album and it's fantastic. For anyone who's wondering what to get for Christmas gifts…it's a good one!!!! Christmas holidays are right around the corner and I'm racking my brain trying to think about gifts this year…I'm the worst about being original in a lot of cases, so I tend to be a gift card giver…okay, not so original. I'm going to attempt making Thanksgiving dinner this year and I've been buying all the *Good Housekeeping* magazines to try to figure the whole thing out…could be a disaster, but I'll give it my best shot.

Anyway, I have an early radio phone interview, so I guess it's about time to hit the hay!!!

December 2, 2002

Well, Thanksgiving came and went, and I managed not to burn down the house. My sister, her husband, and my niece came over. She told me a friend of hers asked where she was going for Thanksgiving, and she said "Terri's," and the friend asked if I would be having it catered...sigh...I think sometimes the public has a bit of a different sense of what our lives are like...at least mine anyway. I had a wonderful relaxing weekend watching movies and catching up with family and friends and planning holiday get-togethers. I LOVE this time of year. I feel like I neglect all of my pals working so much all year long, and Christmas is when I beg for forgiveness and entice them over with food and drink and hope they still love me.

I went to Tootsie's Saturday night and had a great time. We only stayed about an hour or so, 'cause it was really crowded, but I got up and sang a few numbers and it took me back to the days of old. It feels really strange to get up and sing there and actually have people paying attention, and singing my OWN hits now, not everybody else's...oh, what a great feeling. The owner, Steve, came up to me and said, "I tell people they have NO idea the conditions you had to play under down here back then...they have no idea"...well I do, and I'm glad someone else knows. It's gotten a lot better than it was then...it was dangerous to be down there after dark 15 years ago, and I only got paid $15 a day plus tips. When Steve told me what he pays musicians now, I was glad to hear they can at least eat. Anyway...they always seem so proud when I go in and make me feel welcome and at home, and I really appreciate that more than they know. Christmas shopping is on the agenda for today, then it's off to do some writing the rest of the week, and the parade in Knoxville Friday, and show in Earth City, Missouri on Saturday...always plenty to keep me busy.

December 16, 2002

Well, the time is certainly upon us. This has been such a wonderful year in every way, and I have so many blessings to be thankful for. I have a wonderful family, great friends, and some fantastic new people in my professional life. The single has gone top ten just in time for the chart break for 3 weeks over the holidays. I'm anticipating it's going to climb even higher on the chart again when the break is over on Jan. 6th. We're getting great stories about the radio station phones ringing. I guess there are a lot of "Mad" people out there. The record label is leaning towards "Three Mississippi" being the next single. They believe in the song so much it was almost the first single, but I do believe we chose wisely to wait. We have plenty to choose from, so we're grateful to have this kind of dilemma...too many choices are better than not enough. Hopefully we'll get 4 singles from the album by the time it's all said and done, so there'll be plenty of opportunity to get the other songs heard as well. I sent Christmas cards to all the fan club members this year.

When I saw how well they turned out, I couldn't resist. I don't do that every year, but this was one card I couldn't keep to myself!!! I think Oscar makes a great MAX...

December 29, 2002

Well, I was so excited about going to Alberta early for a family ski trip...of all times there wasn't enough snow. We watched the TV ski reports all day and night long...hoping for snow...we almost did a snow dance (which is like a rain dance, only with jingle bells instead of drums). They finally opened the runs in Jasper on Friday the 20th, and off we went to dodge rocks and ski over patches of grass for one day. You gotta be pretty desperate to do that, but we had a good time anyway, just had to be more careful, and not many of the runs were open. I guess we'll try again next year. The saving grace I have is that my CMT "In with the band" is a ski trip in Colorado, so I'll get a second run at it this year...yay!!! I hope the winner can ski, if not, I'll be on the bunny hill with them, but that's okay. We had a great time in the Rocky Mountains just the same, and I had a wonderful Christmas with my family. I've actually managed to get into shape over the holidays...nothing like a new album release around the corner to inspire willpower. We're planning all kinds of neat promos and TV appearances around the album release, including a pending album release party at Tootsie's with the full band, full show. We're trying to figure out how everyone can see it, which may include video screens downstairs and outside, but nothing is set in stone yet…how exciting!!

I have so much to be thankful for…2002 was a wonderful year in every way, and I couldn't have been blessed more. I'm doing a lot of phone interviews over the next week in conjunction with the album release, and have certainly enjoyed the calm before the storm…I'll be gone from home for three weeks straight starting mid-January, but I'm so happy to get out there and kick in the New Year with a busy road schedule…gotta make hay while the sun shines, so they say. I hope everyone has a joyous New Year's Eve, and remembers to be responsible while they're at it…

I'm starting to miss my audience, as we haven't done a show in over three weeks now…withdrawals!!!!! I'm ready to kick some A$$ in '03.

January 6, 2003

My hand is falling off...I have just signed about 700 CD booklets for pre-orders. Countrystars.com says the album has been one of their top pre-sellers...which is very nice to hear. I played the Opry on Friday night, and got to chat with some pals backstage. It was great to get in front of a crowd again, and with a big hit to boot!!! After the broadcast, there was a girl scout troop waiting in the back alley for autographs...I felt like quite the diva with all the little screams...I was trying to figure out what all the fuss was about, so I was checking behind me to see if Lance Bass was coming down the stairs...ahhhhh...to be 12 again. I went to see a TV taping of Allison Moorer at 12th and Porter on Saturday night, and ran into some more music biz pals. Apparently that was the place to be, but I didn't realize it was a TV taping till after I got there, and didn't have a ticket to get in (I thought it was a cover charge), and the people in line said I wouldn't get in without a ticket, so I snuck in the back door...okay, I was desperate. Anyway, she is just great, and I've been a fan for a long time, but this was my first time seeing her live. Her sister, Shelby Lynne, got up to sing with her (another fave of mine), so we all got a two-for-one. This month is going to be busy, but I'm sooooooo ready to play…Billy Bob's here we come!!!!

January 28, 2003

It's certainly been a whirlwind few weeks. It all started with the end of the holidays, and a show in Ft. Worth, Texas, and Billy Bob's on Jan 11th. From there, Greg and I stayed in the area and I got up at 5 a.m. the following Monday in Dallas and started a two day radio, television and overall album promo junket that's still going strong. We flew to Toronto after Dallas and did a whole bunch of television and several print interviews, and the Mike Bullard Show (which is Canada's answer to Letterman). From there we rode the bus overnight back to Nashville. The morning of Jan. 22nd, the Soundscan album numbers came in, and it took all I could not to just faint, throw up, or burst into tears. It was a new record for me...almost 34,000 units the first week, and the highest debut that I've ever had (#5) on the album charts. The news made the rest of the day a joy, and I was on the verge of tears every time someone congratulated me. The *USA Today* feature ran the same day, and the album reviews kept coming in insanely over-the-top great. I've never tried to please critics, but it sure doesn't hurt my feelings when they respond the way they have been. We had two album release parties that night. One was at a place called The Mirror in Nashville at 6 p.m. We played an acoustic set for a Nashville music industry crowd, and it was just great to see all the familiar faces I've come to know over the years. It blew me away to see that many folks show up for the party, and I felt a lot of love and tremendous support from the music community.

From there, we went to Tootsie's Orchid Lounge for the big bash. I couldn't believe the fans who slept outside all night and stood in line all day. It really brings it all home for me to stand on the stage at the place I wandered into and got my first music gig at when I was 18. The memories came flooding back, and the feeling I got standing there with a huge audience jam-packed in there, singing along to all of MY songs, just blew me away...words cannot describe, so I won't even try.

The next day, we did MWL Stars for CMT. We decided to play "Pain to Kill," cause it's the album title cut and a great rocker. I was also feeling a bit vocally stretched from the two previous weeks and "Three Mississippi" was a bit too much of a workout for me that day. It went off without a hitch, and Kevin and I boarded a flight to Las Vegas immediately following the show wrap-up. We got in at around

7 p.m., and the bus (it was already there) picked us up and we had 4 hours to kill before the rest of the band got in, so we went to the Hard Rock. I saw George Clooney in the restaurant and sauntered up and said "Hi" to him…he was very nice, and pretty damn cute too. Then Kevin and I walked around…I was exhausted, but we managed to unwind a bit, and then went back to the bus at around 11:30 and I hit the hay. The rest of the band flew in an hour later…we drove overnight to Sparks, Nevada, and played two sold-out shows…the crowd was probably the best, most energetic casino crowd I've ever seen. We drove all day Sunday to get to Colorado. There was a football game to watch so we killed some time.

Yesterday I got up at 5 a.m. and did a satellite radio tour, then off to Eldora ski resort to meet up with the winner of the "CMT in with the band" show. He is a real sweetheart and an avid skier who taught me a few pointers along the way. I really enjoyed the day, and the CMT cameraman on skis was VERY IMPRESSIVE.

Today we play Greeley, Colorado. I love this state and the people in it. The CMT crew will be at sound check, along with the winner (his name is Lee), and at the show tonight.

Tomorrow morning, another satellite radio tour, then the rest of the day a few interviews, and trying to rest up a bit. Sorry it was so long, but I had some catching up to do.

February 9, 2003

Today I'm at the Konocti Harbor resort in California. Last night we did a show in Oregon for a great crowd. I got some sort of funk in Arizona last week, could have been the climate change, dust, or anything in between. We've gone from one climate to the next on this run, and with all the shows and promo work, I think it just got to me. It's so frustrating when I know I can't sing like I want to and have to skip encores to keep from getting permanent voice damage, but the people last night seemed to understand. Hopefully the next few days off from singing will help me recuperate. We've been out on the road steadily now for quite awhile and I'm starting to miss a normal-sized fridge. Our fridge on the bus has food falling out of it every time we open it.

I went to Seattle on Friday and visited the Lia show and KMPS. We're hoping and praying we can go #1 on Monday with "I Just Wanna Be Mad." It's been a long slow climb and now it's just hold-our-breath and wait-and-see time.

OH MY GAWD…Greg just came to my door and told me that I had a phone call, handed me his cellphone and it was the Mercury Radio promo staff…they said I'm going Number 1 in R&R tomorrow. I walked out of the room and the whole band and crew were outside cheering and popping a champagne cork. I think I'm going to cry. I can't believe it…all the hard work paid off, and now, for the first time since 1998, I have the #1 single…party TIME!!!!!!

March 9, 2003

I found out I'm nominated for Female Vocalist of the Year at this year's ACMs. I must say that at this stage of my career, I'd sort of gotten to the point where I'd come not to expect to be nominated at these awards shows, but I also must say I nearly lost my voice screaming when I found out I had indeed been nominated. Winning is one thing, but just being in the same ranks as the women in this category really, really made me feel like all the years of hard work is finally paying off.

"Three Mississippi" is officially going for airplay on Monday (March 10th) and so far, I'm hearing nothing but great feedback, so hopefully it will follow suit with "Mad."

I've also been really busy painting (yes, painting!) some rooms at home and it's been quite awhile since I've done that, but the experience I have painting for a living way back when, has come in handy.

Other than all of that exciting stuff, I produced a track for the up-and-coming Patsy Cline Tribute album due out soon. My band and

I played our version of "Walking After Midnight" and I sang the lead vocal on the 40th anniversary of Patsy's death…talk about eerie. I used to play many of her songs on the stool at Tootsie's and to have been included on a project with the likes of Natalie Cole, Norah Jones, kd lang and Diana Krall is amazing. Patsy inspired me in more ways than I can ever say. Her recordings contributed so much to my vocal styling, and this was a wonderful opportunity to pay tribute to what she has meant to me.

I remember the only time I ever took something that didn't belong to me. It was an original Patsy Cline album cover (kd lang had scratched her name in at the bottom of it) that hung on the wall of Tootsie's Orchid Lounge for years and years, and this is the first time I have admitted to this, but I took the damn thing one day, 'cause I just had to have it for inspiration. I just kind of walked up the stairs and slid it into my guitar case when nobody was looking. I was 18 years old, and I thought I had just struck gold. Of course I plan on giving it back someday… but for now, it still hangs in my house, and always has, and the folks at Tootsie's say I can keep it!!!!

March 17, 2003

I had to go the record label today to go over some wardrobe choices for the "Three Mississippi" video on Thursday. As I was running down Music Row with all these clothes in hand, I was sure I heard someone yell "GET A JOB!!!!"

With everything going on right now, it's hard to keep things straight. There's a big CMT shoot on Friday for "Ultimate Country Home"...they're giving a house away to one of their viewers and I decorated the dining room. It was fun to spend someone else's money for a change, but now I want to redecorate MY dining room.

I also found out I made the finals for two Flameworthy Video Award nominations for "I Just Wanna Be Mad." Cockiest Video is one of the categories (Best Female Video is the other). I will say this...Shania and I are the only two women in the Cockiest Video Category, and we also happen to both be Canadian. What's interesting is that most people view Canadians as so polite, passive and non-confrontational, so how did we both end up in the "Cocky" category? Beats me.

We're playing the Austin Rodeo again next week and I'm totally jazzed about it. Austin has always been one of my favorite places to go and the music scene is fantastic. I can't wait to hit 6th street after the show.

After finishing the home renovations, I don't care if I ever have another paintbrush in my hand again. I painted my music room/studio Ralph Lauren RED, and by the time I was finished, I looked like I'd just murdered a dinosaur...I went to the corner market to get a beverage and the clerk almost called the cops... I'm not the neatest, most graceful painter, obviously.

We're having the #1 party for "Mad" on Wednesday and it's so exciting to be able to be part of a #1 song again...can't wait.

My mom informs me that her book should be finished sometime by the end of the year...that's right, a BOOK. She's writing about her life, and believe me, it will make for some interesting reading. She's a very strong woman, and I know this book will inspire many people. Well, the phone has been ringing off the hook, so someone is mad at me right now...I'd better go check the caller ID.

April 17, 2003

I know it's been quite a while since I've had time to write, so this will be a long one.

The end of March started off with a long run from the 27th to April 5th up north and in Canada. Our Devils Lake shows went great, and the second show had to have seats added down front because it was oversold. We then went on to Regina, Saskatchewan, and arrived just in time for load-in and sound check...the border crossing took a bit longer than usual as they didn't open till 8 a.m., and we arrived at around 4 a.m., so we had to sit there for four hours. I was asleep anyway, so I didn't even notice. When I woke up, we'd crossed into Saskatchewan and it was nothing but wheatfields for miles...ahhhhh, home sweet home...the prairies. Craig and I were sitting up front (the two lone Canadians) staring out the front window like a couple of homesick fools...looking at...nothing but yellow grass. We looked up into the sky to see a flock of Canada geese in perfect form flying closely together...Craig pointed upward and said

"Look, it's the Canadian Air Force!" I nearly peed my pants...what with the war in Iraq going on and the Canadian government's hesitation to get involved, I found the comment quite interesting, and humorous to say the least...

Our Canadian shows were awesome. My faves were probably Edmonton and Calgary, for two reasons. I got to see family and friends in both places, and *People Magazine* came all the way to Edmonton to interview and do a photo shoot for a feature all about lil ol' me. I'm blown away that I get to be in this magazine, knowing how many people read it...I can't wait to read the article and see the pics of my family and me at home.

My pal Jann Arden introduced me in Calgary, and I must say it was quite a unique intro...in her own unique style...it was great to see Jann again. Then the whole family (aunts, uncles, cousins) went to my grandparents' after the show (in the middle of a snowstorm) and had a birthday party for one of my aunts. It was a late night, and I was beat after doing a show, and then the little party, but it was fun to see everyone.

I flew home to Nashville on the 5th and got ready for the Flameworthy's on Monday night. My call time was 11 a.m. Monday for makeup, and then I did a bunch of press interviews, etc. that afternoon. I saw a whole bunch of big stars and big boobs that night. Hollywood was out in full force to say the least. It was a fun-filled evening of events, and I was able to sign autographs for almost everyone outside the Flameworthy's before the show started. After the show, a few of us ended up at Tootsie's, and I ended up on stage singing to the jam-packed, claustrophobic crowd…they were all too hammered to let the sardine-can-type atmosphere bother them though. Richard Young from the Kentucky Headhunters joined us as well…and I must say what a SWEET man he is. Then I went next door to Robert's Western World and met some of the contestants who were in that new *Nashville Stars* show.

Wednesday the 9th we travelled to L.A. to tape the *Wayne Brady Show*. What a great guy, and I think I was so fatigued at this point that every ounce of nervousness I had was wiped out, so we just had a great time on the show. Then we flew back to Nashville on the 11th and got on the bus that night at midnight to go to Logan, West Virginia. I got up the next day to find us at a hotel in the middle of nowhere (which is really nothing new). I've been keeping up with my fitness routine but couldn't find a treadmill anywhere, so I proceeded to run circles around the hotel, only to be stalked by fifteen 12-year-old girls screaming, "TERRRIIIIII CLAAAAARK!!!" I tell ya, they were too cute. I knew at that moment what it feels like to be

Britney Spears. The poor girl must have hearing aids, cause little girls shrieking can be damaging to one's ears. After taking pictures and signing their scraps of paper, I headed to my room to shower for sound check. After my shower, I came down to the lobby in the elevator to meet the van that was taking us to the theater, and before I even got off the elevator and came round the corner, I could hear these little whispers, saying: "shhhhhh, here she comes...shhhhh, she's coming"...then I came around the corner and BAM...they'd cloned themselves and multiplied into double the group they'd been before, a swarm of pubescent girls shrieking, and screaming, and throwing autograph books at me, all of them dripping wet in their bathing suits and birthday party hats, fresh from the pool...it was a trip.

After we got back from Logan, I did another photo shoot for the *People* story, and then a 4 hour long interview for *Inside Fame*. I'll tell you what, starting from the day you were born and recounting all the gory details of your life is a hard thing to do...I think I almost cried a few times. There'll be a lot that people never knew coming up on this show, and I hope they still like me after they see it. I'm glad I have a good memory for detail...and I gave them a bunch of old footage and home movies, which will be embarrassing as hell, but informative as well.

After all of that, I'm taking the rest of this week off, and will report back after my vacation...ahhhhhhhh.

May 7, 2003

I should probably start posting in my journal a little more often, since I've found out it's going to be published in BOOK form. We got contacted by a publishing company that wants to publish my journal writings and sell them in bookstores all over the continent, and I will even get to sell them at my live shows too...how exciting is that?

On a different note...I just got home from finishing up the dining room for "CMT's Ultimate Country Home," and I must say it looks fab. I went with the Tuscan theme and we even got to make spaghetti and eat it in the dining room after we were finished. Oscar came to help us today, and ate so much Pedigree dog food that he left a gift of his own in the master suite...

Anyway, I'm thrilled to get to be the one who puts on the backyard concert for the winners and friends, and I'm trying to figure out a way that some of my fans can get into the show as well.

The ACMs are right around the corner and we'll be performing "I Just Wanna Be Mad" on the show...I'm finalizing my outfits and such, and having a ball thinking about how much fun mom and I are going to have in Vegas at the show. Whether I ever win or not, it's so awesome to finally be in the running after all these years.

"Three Mississippi" debuted on CMT last week and is starting to get conversions at radio. Although off to a slow start, we all feel optimistic about it picking up speed over the next couple of weeks...phone requests are still the best way to get songs heard, so I'm hoping all my fans are out there burning it up. *Inside Fame* is gathering information, interviewing people, and getting it all together for what's going to be a great show...they flew mom down to Nashville to interview and she even got to stay a whole week (plus an extra day due to weather conditions)...SPEAKING of weather...we've had what I would consider the worst string of storms across the South and Midwest over the past week...I swore the roof was going to blow off the other night, and a lot of people have lost their homes and loved ones...it's so sad, and I hope everyone is praying for them. Mother Nature can be so unpredictable...

May 28, 2003

Well after a whirlwind couple of weeks, I figured it was time for a journal entry. I went to New York on Tuesday May 13th for the *Grace Magazine* party that I was to be singing at on the 14th. Winn and I were the only two who flew up for it, and my manager was to come in the day of the party. I spent most of the flight trying to dodge the drunk guy behind me who kept grabbing my head for leverage every time he stood up….now I know why people fly 1st class. Back to the reason I'm going to New York…This is high fashion, and a different world than us hillbilly singers are used to, so I had no idea what to expect. My pal Jann Arden just happened to be performing in a theater above Studio 54 the same time we were there, and I had the eve of the 13th off, so immediately after getting off the plane, I applied my makeup on the NYC airport curb while Winn held my tiny compact mirror up in front of me…oh the glamour of it all!!! The driver dropped me at Studio 54, and Winn took our luggage to the "W" hotel in Times Square (which was quite SPLENDID). I did a little interview on camera and gushed about Jann, as the Canadian network was there doing a documentary on her...and her show was magnificent...she's funnier than she's ever been, and she played songs from her new record due out soon. She got me up to sing, to a largely UN-country audience...so I did "Empty" and "No Fear," just me and a guitar...the way this whole thing started.

The next day I got in a cab at about 11 a.m. and went shopping for cowboy boots for the ACMs the following week. I found some really cool (and too damn expensive) boots, and found my way back to the hotel. We left for sound check, then went back to do a fitting for the ACMs. Amy Berlin, this wonderful stylist whom I met at the *Grace Magazine* shoot dressed me and she had some great stuff. We ended up going with a jacket that was from the Berkley collection, and I swear I've never seen so many clothes or tried on so many clothes (some of which made me feel a little too...uhm...naked) in my life. We did the show and I wore the cutest (is that a word?) denim thingy that night, and had my outfit all picked out for the ACMs too...feeling like a princess for sure.

Some of the people at the fashion show didn't know who the hell I was, but after I got up and acoustically played a few songs, I think they were really into it...New York has lost their country station and there were several folks in the crowd who were grateful to hear it again...and the other folks were extremely nice and very complimentary. We ended up going to Elaine's, which is a famous hangout for famous people, after the fashion gig, and I had this guy walk up to me as soon as we walked in and say: "uhhhhh....Tewi Cwak...nobody in here knows you except me, but I am a 'UGE fan"...okay, that was my best New York accent...he proceeded to circle the table I was at several times during the evening...just to get a three-dimensional view I guess....hope he wasn't disappointed. Winn and I went back to the Hotel at around 1 a.m., and got some good sleep before departing the next day. I'll continue in my next entry about what the REST of the past two weeks was like...it's too long to go on in this entry...to be continued...

May 29, 2003

Okay, where was I?

We flew home from New York and got into Nashville at around 3:30 that afternoon. We had to be at the bus at 7:30 that evening to roll on to Maryland. When I got to the bus, Winn was already in his bunk fast asleep. We got to Maryland and did the show that night. It was a good crowd, and Mark Wills was also on the bill with us. We then went on to North Carolina to do a show with Alan Jackson on Saturday. After the show, we headed back to Nashville, arrived home the next day, and I started packing my stuff for Las Vegas and the ACMs. My mom, dad, uncle and aunt had already left Edmonton (DRIVING!!!) on Friday night to get to Vegas on Sunday. We flew to Vegas Monday morning, to get there in time for our first rehearsal Monday night. Mom and company picked me up at the airport and we all went to lunch with my PR wiz Holly, and had Mexican food at the Pink Taco….yes, you heard me right.

After lunch, I played some nickel slots with the family and heard all about their adventurous

29-hour drive from Canada. If Vegas had to depend on us for its income, it would have been a ghost town many moons ago…the Clarks are known for keeping a tight grip on the purse strings.

I was able to get the whole family into the rehearsal, got to visit with Reba a bit, haven't talked to her in years, so of course I was all giddy and goofy…I will always turn into a 15-year-old fan club member around her and Wynonna. At one point, Rac Clark AND Dick Clark came over to say hello, so there were more Clarks in that room than you could shake a stick at. I went through my rehearsal and just stood there looking back at the band saying… we're FINALLY here!!!!! It's taken 8 years, but here we ARE!!!!!

The next day, I was up at the crack of dawn doing radio interviews at the remotes they had set up at another hotel. That stuff went on all day long, I did a final fitting for my clothes at 4:30 that afternoon, and after that went off to a dinner for radio that the record label was throwing. I stayed for about an hour at that shindig, then went to bed…I wanted to be rested and sound good on the show. The next day, I had breakfast and got my stuff together, then headed over for dress rehearsal. That went well, and it was only hours until the show started. I kept thinking about all those years I sat in front of the TV watching this show, and now I was up for the big award we all dream about as singers. They had my performance pretty close to the beginning of the show and I sat beside mom in the audience. Once the performance was over, it was easier to relax and enjoy the rest of the show. We had a great time on that stage, and I just looked at the fans the whole time, 'cause they are always my inspiration, I was so glad they had a mosh pit of fans there this year…it really set me at ease. We rocked and I was so pleased with how it all went, as was everyone else. I didn't win Female Vocalist, but, as Wy told me…"God has his own time, and your time will come when it's right." My dressing room was shared by Martina and Wynonna, and Reba's was right beside ours, so I was quite giddy that whole day…very emotional in many ways. The after-party was just as fun…I got up with my band and did "Love Me Like a Man," and "The Rock Encore Medley"…what a blast. We got on the plane back to Nashville the next day, after pigging out on McDonald's and Krispy Kremes, and got on the bus that same night to go to Anderson, South Carolina, where I did an in-store for Wal-Mart, then a show with Trace Adkins…by this time I'm feeling the need to STOP for a few days, and there is relief in sight. We went on to Fanning Springs after that and played a very HOT sticky show for a very enthusiastic crowd. When the bus rolled into Nashville on Sunday, I decided it was time to just REST for awhile…ya think????

June 5, 2003

Well, I just finished going through all the wonderful gifts all my fans brought to the fan club party for me. I must say, over the years it seems people have recognized the things I like and enjoy the most...and it blows me away how kind everyone has been. One of the highlights was this awesome ring that the fan club had made for several members, as well as one for me...it really touched my heart and I cannot express enough how much everyone's thoughtfulness means to me. Every letter and gift has been opened, and is near and dear to my heart because it came from the people for whom I REALLY make the music. I'm also always taken aback by every individual who tells me what the music has meant to their lives. I agree every artist has fans, some of whom belong to multiple fan clubs and we all think OURS are the best and most loyal, but there's just something very special about the family of friends we have accumulated over the past 8 years. I did the entire show, and was glad I did, 'cause there was one lady who came all the way from Spain and had NEVER seen a show, so she left very satisfied that she'd finally gotten to see what she reads about on the message board. I came home (after debating a Tootsie's stop) and relaxed, opened gifts, and just chilled out for the evening with Oscar and all of his ceramic look-alikes…my place is beginning to look like a weiner-dog shrine…

This morning I was up at 6 a.m. and went to do some radio morning drive-time interviews… it took a long time to wake up today for some reason, but we all had a blast talking to the folks in different parts of the country via remote. There were two boxes of fresh original Krispy Kremes and I ate 5 of them, along with a Dwight Yoakam biscuit…yummy, but not a good thing for the ass…oh, the joys of zero willpower. I play a 20-minute set at the Universal show tonight at the big stadium, then it's off to Waco tomorrow to play the Cattle Barons Ball on Saturday night.

Until next time…staying away from doughnuts.

June 6, 2003

I've really been burning up the journal lately with all the exciting things going on. The Universal show at the stadium last night went great...I love it when we get a chance to play for so many people at one time, but 20 minutes felt like it went by way too fast for me...we were just getting started!

I was up this morning at 6 a.m. for some radio remotes down at the convention center. I don't think I've had so many other artists compliment me on one of my songs as have about "Three Mississippi"...even radio is telling me that other artists are talking to them about it...that just made me feel awesome. The capper though, was when WYNONNA walked in, and the first thing out of her mouth is..."Your new single is great...love it!" Well I just thought I was gonna pass out right there...I mean this was coming from someone who influenced and inspired me so much when I was a kid...those words meant the world to me. After hearing that, I need to wait for something REALLY cool to happen before I do another journal entry...

Edmonton, Alberta, April 1, 2003
Photographer: Jim Wells